Please Tell Me I'm On Mute

ROMI BRENNER

ISBN: 0-9798749-1-2

ISBN-13: 9780979874918

Cover photo by Jennifer Margolis

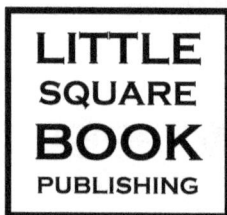

**LITTLE
SQUARE
BOOK
PUBLISHING**

www.littlesquarebook.com

For my children,

who fill my heart with a joy I cannot put into words,

and for my husband,

without whom they would only be a dream.

CONTENTS

If evolution really works, how come mothers only have two hands? ~Milton Berle

PLEASE TELL ME I'M ON MUTE

"Tell them you're holding a rabbit!"

I gave my daughter a tiny nod and benign smile, the one I vowed I would never give her, the one that says "I'm not really listening but I'm acknowledging that you spoke to me."

"Tell them! Tell them you're holding a baby rabbit!" she said again, hopping around me. I realized I was still bouncing the stuffed animal bunny over my left shoulder and patting it on the back, in the auto-pilot manner that all parents permanently do after they've had babies, regardless of whether the object being rocked is an actual baby or a sack of flour or pillow.

I held up my hand, craning to hear the person talking. One of the advantages of modern technology is the ease of attending conference calls from home. Since most of my work team is on the east coast and I am on the west, this perk makes the 6:00 and 7:00 a.m. calls a lot more palatable. It also means that my daughter is home with me at that time and she seems to have considerably less regard for the fact that I'm on the phone than I do.

Upon catching up with enough of the diatribe to know what was going on, I held up my finger in front of my lips and mouthed "sssshhhhh" to Mia.

"Tell them, Mom," she breathed in a loud stage whisper. She was now sitting on my left foot, her legs and arms wrapped around my leg like a koala bear. Bless her, my daughter doesn't seem to understand that whispering is still talking, and a small child's stage whisper is about as subtle as a bull in a china shop.

I hit the mute button. "Love," I sighed, "When I'm on early morning phone calls, if you want to sit with me while I'm on the line you have to be completely quiet, or else you have to leave the room."

"Okay," she agreed solemnly. She unwrapped herself from her perch and I turned my attention back to the call. The discussion was getting a little more heated and I waited for the person talking to finish before jumping in.

"We got the estimate and it seems really high," I said. Silence. Thinking I'd offended someone, I hastened to explain. "I'm sure everyone was following protocol, but given how simple this seems to fix, this dollar amount seems really inflated." Still nothing. Then I remembered I was on mute. I quickly hit the button and repeated my statements. The conversation resumed, and opinions about the finer points of programming fixes and their equivalent price tags were batted around.

For a while my concentration was such that all background noise was successfully filtered out. However, the sound of chirpy singing began to get unmistakably louder. It wasn't a specific song, just something Mia was composing as she went, in a full-bodied operatic style. I hit the button again.

"MIA!" I hissed. And then in a stage whisper of my own, "*COMPLETELY* quiet! That means singing as well."

She winked and gave me the thumbs up, accompanied by a big nod. I winked back, hit the mute button again and turned my attention back to the call. It wasn't even a minute before I heard the screeching sound of a chair being carelessly dragged across the floor.

There was no point even saying anything. Kids are so literal that in order to get my child to be utterly silent, I would've had to have said "Don't talk, shout, yell, scream, sing, whisper, hammer, throw things, play the drums, play your kazoo, use your battery operated toys, drag things across the floor, stomp around, be an army commando, be a cheerleader, leap off the furniture, be a jungle cat..." etc, etc, etc, ad infinitum.

Furthermore, this kind of request, besides requiring more time to explain than the duration of the actual phone call, wasn't a fair demand to place upon a little girl who, due to her age, simply wouldn't be able to comply.

I left the room and went upstairs instead. "We did turn in the BRD," I said. "We sent it about two weeks ago. Should I resend it?"

"We didn't receive it," confirmed our developer.

"No problem," I said. "I'll resend it. Does anyone else want a copy?"

The door creaked open slowly. I spun around to find Mia on the floor on all fours, crawling her way over to me with her meanest lion snarl. I frowned and instantly put my finger up to my lips. She nodded.

The lioness continued to stalk me as the team on the call confirmed the recipients of the business requirements document and went over the timeline for the project. Suddenly Mia scampered off, leaving the door wide open.

"As soon as we get the BRD we will begin work on the high level design," the developer said, wrapping up the status of my project. "Does anyone have any other questions or can we move on?" We came to a consensus that there was nothing more to add, and the next project was up for discussion.

As quickly as they had gone, the footsteps returned, getting rapidly louder as Mia galloped back into the room.

"I JUST MADE A POO ALL BY MYSELF IN THE BIG GIRL TOILET!!!!" she boomed.

Her eyes were gleaming with pride, her smile as wide and deep as my abject horror.

Was I still on mute?! The team on the call was deep in another debate, and since I was not connected with this project at all, there was no reason for me to jump in with a remark to test if they could hear me. The fact that no one was laughing or didn't say anything about it wasn't a definitive indicator, and I didn't want to draw attention to this statement just in case, due to some preposterous miracle, that even if I wasn't muted they might not have heard it. I drew in a deep breath and just shook my head.

Mia was confused.

Potty training came late for this child, and was a desperate battle fought ardently on both sides until her eventual surrender. The final cutting of the potty training cord was protracted further by her insistence for many more moons that I sit with her in the bathroom while she jettisoned her undesirables. Therefore, a solo trip like this was usually cause for much celebration, or at the very least an encouraging "YEAH!"

I weakly gave her the thumbs up and hoped the gurgling echoes of the flush down the hall was not the sound of my career literally going down the toilet as well.

I put my finger over the speaker on the phone this time and calmly whispered to her, "Please. Please. For the love of God. Please let's play the quiet game until Mommy is off the phone."

Mia smiled conspiratorially and promptly held up her finger over her wide grin. But this round was already over and she had won by a landslide. However, tomorrow is another day. Let the games begin.

NOW I'M THE MOMMY

We were still in the hospital, recovering. Me, from the surgery that had separated my baby from my womb, and her, from the trauma of being wrenched from it.

It was late at night and the doctors were concerned about my daughter's rapid respiration.

"We've found that babies often do better when they're with their moms," said the nurse, "Let's try having her lay next to you."

My husband was instantly at attention. "What if she rolls over?" he asked, referring to me.

The nurse and I both assured him that the bloated, beached whale that had replaced my body wasn't going anywhere without assistance. The nurse showed me how to form a cradle with my left arm and she gently lowered in my little bundle.

My infant fit in the crook of my arm like a puzzle piece. Her warm, silken head rested on my shoulder, and her tiny toes nudged my fingers. Her cuddly little body and the blanket swaddling it molded into the space next to my ribs so that we were flush up against each other, her right ear next to my heart.

Within seconds, her breathing slowed and she took in deep, calm air. At the same time, I felt my own tension go, and my daughter's serene, rhythmic breath mimicked my own.

My husband and I were astounded at how quickly it worked. As we gazed at our child, a profound understanding settled in my bones.

Now *I* was the Mommy. The person who will have to make it all better. The person who will have to know what time is bedtime, or that the baby needs a coat today, or how much toothpaste to use for a sixteen month old, or that it's okay to have her friends for a sleep over tonight. I was now the subject matter expert on a person I had known for two days.

I looked at this sleeping little cherub whose trust in me was absolute. Did she have a clue that I had no idea what I was doing? That I didn't know how to kiss booboos or chase away the monsters under the bed? Could she sense that I had never lullabied a baby to sleep? Or strapped one into a car seat?

But here she was, whole and pure and relying on me to come through for her and be able to do this.

It was this day I learned what I could never had fathomed before I felt another human life grow inside my body, before I saw my fetus waving in utero on the ultrasound. Before I held a head the size of a grapefruit in my hands. Before I found myself hoping for nothing more in the world than to see my baby simply take another breath.

What I learned was this: there is an aching abyss of love that opens for every new parent. It is ardently protective and infinitely patient. It is to fill with hope and dreams for someone else, to instinctively know that you will always put this little person before yourself.

Having a baby was like flying first class. Sure, you'll still get there if you fly in the back with everyone else. But once you recline your spacious seat all the way back while you sip your wine from a glass, and enjoy your freshly made salad on a real plate, you realize what you've been missing. Having a baby was like being let in on a secret; now a whole world had opened up, and I knew I would never be able to go back to the way it was before.

I realized that now I wasn't just me anymore.

I was somebody's mother.

HOW TO LEAVE THE HOUSE WITH A NEWBORN

What was it the nurse said? Go easy on yourself, you've just had a baby. Especially in the beginning, even seemingly small things like getting a shower in during the day will be a huge accomplishment.

I was incredulous. What kind of lazy, pathetic bum couldn't even manage a shower in the course of an entire day?! I would be on maternity leave, free all day, practically on vacation for three months! How does a grown woman not find fifteen minutes in a day to bathe and make herself presentable?! This was preposterous, and I was openly disparaging about it, feeling pity and contempt for these self-indulgent, unambitious new moms who sat around on the couch all day, unable to tear themselves away from the TV long enough to do something as small as a basic cleanliness routine.

The universe soon threw my haughty scorn for this idea back in my face with gigantic peals of mocking laughter.

Until you have actually had a newborn in your

midst, there is no way to possibly begin to understand how little time you will have to yourself and how much effort it will take to do something as seemingly simple and mundane as say, leave the house.

When you are just you, and responsible for only the clothes on your own back and possibly your wallet and car keys as well, going out is a concept that requires as much thought and planning as blinking.

However, when there is a new baby in your life and you suddenly find yourself half an hour late for everything, having broken a sweat just getting out the door, you begin to understand that perhaps the nurse did know a thing or two after all. That taking a shower while juggling a new baby is, indeed, something to hang your hat – or towel - on at the end of the day.

For me, it all went a little like this…

The baby finally falls asleep.
Run to the bathroom.
Turn on the shower.
Nod off leaning against the shower waiting for the water to heat up.
Jolt awake, completely disoriented and drooling slightly, when your shoulder slides off shower door.
Step into the shower. Feel the warm water running down your back and hmmmmmrph…
Jolt awake again when your head hits the back of the shower wall.
Finish up in the shower.
Dry off.

Try on seven pairs of jeans, managing to button none of them.

Throw the jeans on the floor in disgust and put on the one remaining clean pair of maternity pants.

Begin blow drying your hair.

Decide to forget it and throw your hair back in ponytail.

Open the diaper bag and begin packing:

> Diapers
>
> Wipes
>
> Diaper rash cream
>
> Bags for throwing away dirty diapers
>
> Several small, fluffy critters to amuse the baby
>
> Portable changing pad
>
> 2 bottles filled with water
>
> Enough formula for 2 feedings
>
> 4 extra binkies
>
> Extra pair of baby socks
>
> Extra onesie
>
> Receiving blanket
>
> Banana for yourself

Go put the diaper bag in the car.

Hear the baby crying.

Get your little bundle out of the crib and hold her for a minute. Coo to the baby as she bobbles her head about your shoulder and starts nibbling on your neck.

Put the baby gently on changing table and continue cooing as you change her diaper.

Smile at your baby while you snap her onesie back together and then pick her up.

Realize you were off a few snaps and now the baby can't straighten her leg.

Put the baby back on changing table and refasten her onesie.

The baby is hungry and begins wailing.

Take the baby downstairs and attempt to make a bottle without her seeing.

The baby spies the bottle and goes ballistic.

Sit down with the baby on the couch and feed her the bottle.

Listen to the sweet sounds of contented gulping and be at peace with the world as you gaze lovingly into her dreamy eyes.

Feel the hot surge of pee on your leg.

Finish feeding the baby and burp her.

Walk upstairs with wet, rapidly cooling pants clinging to your thigh.

Place the baby on the changing table and change her diaper.

Attempt to get the onesie over your baby's head without letting the soiled garment touch her skin.

The baby gets cold and begins fussing.

Put a clean onesie on the baby, carefully wrestling flailing arms and legs into the outfit.

Place the baby on her back on your bed and peel off wet pants.

Throw your pants in the hamper and, too tired to get back in the shower, wash your leg in the sink.

Try on four of the seven pairs of jeans again, just in case any of them fit now.

Throw them on the floor again in disgust.

Locate a pair of ratty sweatpants and decide they are going to have to suffice.

Place a burp cloth over your shoulder.

Scoop up the baby and head downstairs.

Wriggle into your shoes.

Open the door to the garage.

The baby gives a burp like a 250 pound man after chugging a forty ounce can of beer and spits up all over the part of your shirt that is not covered by the burp cloth.

Close the door, kick off your shoes.

Take the baby back upstairs and put her back down on the bed.

Look for a clean shirt.

Find nothing.

Raid your 6'4" husband's drawer and put on one of his long sleeved shirts.

Roll the sleeves up 4 times.

Go back downstairs with the baby and put your shoes on again.

Hear loud eruption noise as the baby has massive diaper blowout.

Kick your shoes off again.

Head back upstairs and place the baby on the changing table.

Consider cutting off the outfit but deftly maneuver it off the baby.

Use half a box of wipes extricating waste from your baby's back, bottom and the rolls on her legs.

Realize there is poo all over the changing table when the baby puts her foot in it.

Holding the baby's foot with one hand, remove the changing table cover out from underneath baby with the other.

The baby objects to being captured and cries.

Know you're never supposed to leave a baby unattended, but know also that she is 3 weeks old and you have a handful of crappy linen.

Strap the baby to the changing table and dash into the bathroom.

Fling the dirty stuff into the sink and dash back to the baby's bedroom.

The baby has peed in your absence and the changing table has a small yellow puddle in the middle of it.

Sop up the pee and use the other half of the box of wipes to clean the baby.

Put a clean diaper and onesie on the baby and head back downstairs.

Put on your shoes and go out the door.

Place the baby carefully into her car seat and tuck her tiny arms and legs into the straps.

Buckle the five-point harness.

Tuck the thick, soft blanket around the baby who has fallen sleep.

Start up the car and back out of the driveway.

Get to the 2nd traffic light before the store and remember you forgot to pack your wallet into the diaper bag.

Do a U-turn at the light and head home.

Run inside to get your wallet.

Fish around in your "regular" bag for two minutes, and curse like a sailor when you don't find the wallet.

Go back to the car and just for grins, dig in the diaper bag again.

Find the wallet at the bottom of the bag.

Start up the engine and back up again.

The baby wakes up hungry, and starts howling.

Get to end of street and turn around and go home as the baby is screaming like someone cut off one of her hands.

Take the baby out of the car.

Go make another bottle and flop down on couch with the baby.

Satisfied, the baby falls asleep.

The phone rings and wakes the baby as answering machine records the booming voice of a telemarketer telling you about the adults-only timeshare units available.

Weigh laughing against crying and decide you're too tired to do either one.

Calm the baby and get her back to sleep.

Place the baby in the swing and crawl over to couch.

Feel your eyes close as the sandman bonks you over the head.

Make a mental note right before you drift off to sleep that a perk of living in these times is ordering online delivery service.

Hear popping noises from the baby's lower region.
Pretend you didn't hear and let yourself fall asleep.
It will all be there when you wake up…

GLAZED AND DAZED

In a statement of flagrant contradiction to the widely-accepted mantra of my gender, I confess to being someone who would rather eat a mango for dessert than a piece of chocolate cake. No, really, I say that without so much as a trace of snarkiness and I have never been diagnosed with a mental illness.

It's just that life with a metabolism as efficient as a clogged drain has taught me to look beyond processed sugar to satisfy my sweet tooth. Thus, I have truly come to be one with all things fresh and peeled.

So when Krispy Kreme came to town and people pined in line for hours for their free doughnut while they waited to place their orders, I didn't feel the slightest draw to waste my precious time and expand my waist. In fact, I felt a faintly smug pang of pity for these crowd-followers who demonstrated such a blatant lack of self control.

Indeed, I resisted even going in there for a good long while without so much as a smidge of remorse.

Armed with the conviction that these completely nutritionally-devoid confections were no match for my iron resolve, I felt absolutely safe to go in one morning on my way to work, and pick up a box for my team to say thank you for helping me out on a project.

And, just in case there was any danger of slipping, I casually reminded myself on the way in that when they asked if I'd like my free doughnut I would simply say no thanks.

I opened the door and the very air in the place seduced my nostrils with a sugary smog. I went to the back of the line and ogled the assembly line in fascination. As we meandered along the curved splashguard, I could see the raw dough plopping into the boiling oil, all pale and full of potential as the doughnuts hatched, bobbing to the surface like newborn ducklings learning to swim.

I eyed one in particular as the conveyor belt expertly flipped it onto its back, exposing its evenly deepened, golden brown belly. I reassured myself that my interest was merely journalistic in nature and that I had no attachment to the tanned, puffing pastry.

The line was moving quite quickly and I saw my doughnut get pulled under the glaze waterfall, emerging seconds later with a smooth coating of shiny, opaque icing.

Before I even had a chance to blink, a seemingly disembodied hand had scooped up my doughnut with a piece of wax paper and thrust it, hot and gooey and incredibly soft, into my unsuspecting paw.

Reeling from the shock of abrupt ownership of this confection melting in my palm, I held my ground. It would be rude to throw it out right in front of them. Option B seemed more practical: just wait for my box and then add it to the mix.

As I reached the front of the line, I heard the shake in my voice as I procured 2 dozen of these delicacies; imperceptible to the cashier who didn't know me, yet I recognized the telltale signs of cracks beginning to show. The sultry pastry in my hand was rapidly sending tingling sensations of warmth up into my arm.

I stood back to wait for my name and leaned against a pole for support, breathing a little shallowly. The allure of this doughnut was starting to overwhelm my senses and I heard the alarm bells go off in my head. I couldn't remember when last I'd succumbed to one of these on the food table at work, but I had never before held such a fresh, flawless specimen in my own clutches.

Suddenly the noise in the background faded away and there were only two of us in this world: my doughnut and me. And I knew with everything I had and everything I was, that I had to have it, right there, right then. This need was bigger than both of us, and responding with a primal urge to this culinary kismet, my eyelids fluttered closed as I frantically raised it to my mouth and sank my teeth into its light, fluffy flesh.

I vaguely heard myself groan out loud as my whole world filled with glazed happiness. Like the utter surrender of a roller coaster ride I was powerless to stop, and I devoured the object of my desire in four

21

ravenous, rapturous bites. Upon discovering the deed was over, and not caring who was watching me, I licked the paper to prolong the ecstasy, and seriously considered eating that as well.

Back then, I thought it was incredibly fortuitous timing that they called my name at that precise point, but in hindsight they probably bumped up my order to prevent me from turning on the napkins and chairs as well.

I staggered out of Krispy Kreme with my parcel of lovelies, and did manage to actually get to work before inhaling another one. In a desperate, weak attempt to recapture the moment, I gave in to two more during the day. However, they were meaningless and empty, mere imposters that, while resembling the original in shape and texture, fell miserably short of fulfilling the moment of passionate perfection that had ensued just a few hours earlier.

So, I have resumed avoiding doughnuts like a typhoid ward. But occasionally as I spoon fruit salad onto my plate at hotel lobby breakfast buffets and office potlucks, I secretly smile, dreaming of the doughnut that once ignited my taste buds and made me pillage it with such reckless abandon.

My sweet beloved, we will always have Friday morning.

BED TIME

It was getting late when we climbed into bed. We were organized: sippy cup of water on the nightstand, binky in hand and Sandra Boynton's *Philadelphia Chickens* CD on softly in the background.

"Okay Mia, what do we do?" I asked. "Go to sleep and…?"

"Close eyes!" She grinned and dove into the pillows.

There was a bit of scuffling as she decided on which side of the bed she wanted to lie. I was relegated to Daddy's pillow while she flip flopped on mine for a minute or two.

"No, Mommy, get off!" She pushed my head up and shoved me off the feathers. "You go on this one," she pointed to my side of the bed.

I obliged and we switched. Five seconds later.

"No, Mommy, *this* one!" She pointed back at Russell's pillow.

"We can switch but that's it, Mia, no more changing."

"Okay."

The transaction occurred and was followed by more thrashing for several more minutes.

Finally all was calm.

I was then serenaded by the most touching rendition of "You Are My Sunshine" I had ever heard.

"You are my sunshine, my only sunshine, you make a happeeee....when skies are gway...you never know deaaaah...amuch a love yooooooooo..." On "you" she touched my nose with her index finger, just as I do when I sing it to her, "Pease don't take a sunshine aaaawayyy."

She repeated this several times before moving on to Snuggle Puppy. She punctuated her singing by taking my face in her hands and giving me huge kisses.

Despite the quiet version of a different song in the background, she was consistently in tune and her sweet little voice filled my heart with a mixture of love, joy, happiness, amusement and more love until I thought it was literally going to burst. I could feel I was grinning like a cheshire cat. I didn't want her to think I was laughing at her, but she was just SO incredibly cute I could barely contain myself and let out the occasional silent chuckle when she turned her head to the ceiling on the "oooooooooooooooooos."

Old McDonald was next: "Old MaDonald had a phwarm...eei eei o..." Her enunciation was crisp and very exaggerated on the "eei eei o." "And on a phwarm he had a duck and on a phwarm he had a cow...wuack wuack evywhere moo moo evywhere wuack wuack

wuack wuack."

She interrupted herself to find her binky. I pretended to help her find it so that I could tickle her in the ribs. She giggled and wriggled around.

"Is it here?" I asked and "checked" her neck and delectable cheeks. More giggling.

We located the errant binky and our gorgeous singing session drew to a close.

"What wonderful singing, Mia!" I exclaimed, and I meant it. "You know a lot of songs for someone your age," I told her earnestly. "You're such a clever girl!"

"Hmm," she agreed.

"Okay, pumpkin, time to go to sleep, close your eyes," I told her.

Mia wriggled under the covers until they were up to her nose.

"Cozy!" she beamed and hugged herself.

I rubbed her tiny back and caught a fading glimpse of the baby she used to be just a blink ago. It was way past her bedtime but she would get to sleep in and stay home with Daddy tomorrow. So I snuggled up next to her to inhale her sweet little self while I still can. Her skin was buttery soft and her huge curls brushed my face like a silk scarf.

I find it hard to believe that I will ever be as content again as I was in that very moment, and I recorded this perfect blip in time with my soul, hoping its eternal essence will always store the wholeness of it.

Mia flipped onto her back and rubbed her eyes. It really was time for bed now and "Silly Lullaby" was drawing to a close.

I crooned along softly with the last line, and Mia and I smiled at each other. "Come my baby, time to go in your crib," I told her.

Before she had a chance to protest, I scooped her up in my arms and she grinned.

"I'm a bundle!" she said, and I rocked her gently back and forth as we walked to her room. "It's dark!" she observed as we entered her room.

"Yes it is," I agreed. "That's because it's late."

I put her down in her crib and she hugged her little pillow.

I covered her with her blankie and she asked for Ila Lula.

"I la lula lula lula baby," I began. She interrupted me.

"Baby Baby!" she corrected.

I sang the requested melody over and over, more softly with each verse, and gently massaged her head. Her eyelids finally fluttered closed.

"I love you, my baby, sleep well and sweet dreams," I whispered.

"Okay, bye," she murmured back.

I closed the door and marveled at how lucky I am to be blessed with this unique little girl, and how of all the billions of mothers in the world, I get to be the one to do this with her every night.

I also know I don't have to travel to the ends of the earth to find a sense of purpose and inner peace. It's just a few feet away down the hall.

GERIATRIC BRIDESMAID

Lavender, eggplant, baby pink, black, red, bubblegum pink, sky blue, silver, chocolate brown, and beige with black flowers. If I'd kept every one of my bridesmaid dresses, I would have an assortment of gowns spanning these shades, some of which were repeated a few times. While it is a novelty for most people to be in a wedding or two, for me it became unusual to find myself in the nuptial bleachers with the rest of the guests as opposed to front and center at the altar, next to the bride.

My bridesmaid career began at the age of twenty two, and now, at the ripe age of thirty three, I found myself back in the satin saddle at the bridal store. While it was a very sweet gesture that I was asked to be in the wedding party, I was getting a little long in the tooth to be wearing taffeta.

One of the saleswomen approached me. I like her instantly; she had a kind face and didn't eye me up and down with a sneer of disgust on the corners of her mouth like the last woman at this very shop had done just a few months before.

"Can I help you?" she smiled.

"Yes, please," I replied, wanting this shopping trip to be over as quickly and painlessly as possible. I already knew I was going to cheat. I had been given the freedom to choose the style, as long as it was short. My post-baby body more closely resembled a tree trunk than the hour glass it had been before and the short dresses were just not cut to flatter my new form. I was going to find a long dress and cut gads of it off the bottom.

Within seconds I found myself standing in front of racks of satin, gauzy overlays, and rhinestones. The sample dresses hung like a displaced box of Crayolas, with sizes ranging from 2 – 26. I began grabbing everything that could be made in the required shade of blue.

The saleswoman returned and asked if she could start a fitting room for me. I gratefully handed her the billowing yards of cloth and she disappeared. She returned as I was grabbing the last of the samples.

"I've started your dressing room on the left side, it's number 13," she said helpfully and then added, "Janet will be there to assist you."

I was more than a little panicked at the prospect of Janet (or any other human being with eyes in her head) being privy to the unfortunate flesh that lurks beneath my shirt.

I thanked the woman and scurried to the dressing room, praying silently to evade the hapless Janet. On my way I spied a young nymph of a bride, her twelve-year-old-boy-like body clad in a vision of white with red trim. I wanted to ask her what she was doing out so late on a school night.

I closed the door to my chamber of horrors and the games began. The first dress was a nightmare of cheap, lilac satin. I took off my fleece and jeans and left my socks on in a small act of defiance. My stomach flopped out in a revolting flabalanche of spent skin. I climbed into the dress and attempted to rearrange the plummeting neckline.

I spun around to see myself in the mirror and it was then that I remembered the practical joke that is a bridal shop fitting room. The mirror is on the *outside*. So, if I was to assess the damage, I would have to open the door and be visible to everyone in the store. I cracked the door open and to my relief, found that the only people in the vicinity were the child-bride, who had her hair up in a makeshift bun with one hand and was fluffing wisps of tulley veil with the other, and her attending saleswoman, whose eyes were firmly glued to her charge.

I opened the door and tentatively ventured out. I was standing in a puddle of purple, my luminously white skin even more sallow next to the pastel shades of this Niagara Falls of fabric. I willed the flabalanche to retreat but it stood its gelatinous ground relentlessly. Barf.

And so it went with the halter neckline, the rusched A-line, and the dress with the wide sash under the bust line. Barrrrrrrf.

I was getting a little desperate now, I knew I would have to choose one of these but each was less flattering than the last and I toyed with the idea of just picking one and ordering it in my size without even trying it on.

But there was one in my peripheral vision that beckoned with a heart-flutteringly tempting hint of promise. It was a Grecian-looking number with an empire waistline, made of softly flowing chiffon. It had spaghetti straps that crisscrossed ever so slightly in the back. There was a token band of beading but it was manageable and at this stage of the proceedings, hardly noticeable in comparison to the prom-queen bows and sashes. It helped that the sample dress was apple red, a color that compliments my skin tone rather than make me look like the undead.

I put it on, praying out loud this time that this one would work as I sensed tears were not far behind if it didn't. I stepped out again and BINGO! We had a winner, Ladies and Gentlemen!!!! While nothing that would upstage Halle Berry on Oscar night, it was a respectable gown and I would not have to fight with the flabalanche all night in it. Plus, I could whack four feet off the bottom of it and leave the line intact.

Just for grins, there was one last creation I hadn't tried on so, a glutton for punishment, I figured why not. As I was about to take my last trip to the hall of shame, I heard raucous shrieking emanating from outside the changing room. I froze as a gaggle of twenty-something sylphs gushed over the brideling as if she'd just struck gold.

"THAT'S THE ONE!!!" They were almost hysterical and there was a stampede of young girls outside my flimsy haven walls.

I was trapped. And conflicted. A small, sadistic part of me wanted to go out there with my head held high and show these young bombshells what awaited them in another ten years. But the overriding part of me that felt like a warthog in the field of gazelles kept me breathlessly paused for them to dissipate so that I could sneak a peek and get the hell out of there.

"I LOVE it!!!" "It's so perfect!!" The squealing continued for a good few minutes before they finally went back to change.

I seized the opportunity and threw open the door to see the frump in the mirror in a sateen tent that defied the laws of physics and somehow made my waist look even bigger than my bust.

And… scene.

Recently, I had considered vying for the Guinness Book of World Records. Just a few more weddings and I think I might have had a shot. But today as I pulled these garments over the head of this latte-drinking, corporate-operations-managing, nursery rhyme-singing mom, I realized there comes a point where the ship has sailed. Even though I imagine I was probably fairly close to the prize, this geriatric bridesmaid was now seriously considering tossing her bouquet for good.

ALL HAIL THE FLEECE VIXEN

Six weeks after the accident, when the pain in my spine was so bad that I couldn't sit or stand for more than a few minutes, I decided it was time to go and get sorted out.

The x-rays showed that while there were no fractures, my seized muscles were pulling my spine towards the left, in a weird, 2-D snaking scoliosis.

While setting up the physical therapy appointments, I had specified to the person on the phone that I felt more comfortable seeing a woman. With the problem being my back, I figured my therapist would be getting an eyeful of more than just my scapula and at the ripe age of twenty four, was a bit self-conscious.

At the first visit, my female therapist took a careful history, then stood up, asked me to remove all my clothing from the waist up and lie down on the bench. She closed the door behind her as she left and I quickly obliged. Expecting her melodious voice when the door opened again, I was a bit taken aback by the deep, gruff hello. I popped my head up to find that Ms. Therapist had grown about ten inches taller, sprouted a five o'clock shadow and traded in one of her X chromosomes for a Y.

I was really annoyed at this breach of my specific request and was a little uneasy through the small talk. However, as soon as he started working my pitiful lats, all inhibition flew out the window. The magic in his hands was such instant relief that this man could have strapped me, topless as the day I was born, to a fence post on the interstate during the treatment and I wouldn't have cared.

Over the next month, I returned twice a week for exercises, hot and dreaded cold packs and then the sweet dessert for my efforts: a glorious massage to finish the appointment.

At the end of the ninth session, I was feeling fabulous. The massage was over and I rose from the table slowly, still reeling from the kneady nirvana. I got dressed in a happy daze, gathered my things and headed out to the lobby.

I smiled dreamily at the receptionist, who smiled knowingly back. With a bounce I had forgotten was possible, I bobbed out of the clinic, reborn.

It was still fairly early on a Saturday morning and I decided to grab life by the horns and get all my errands done before I went home. My first stop was the bank. There was a small line and I took my place in the queue.

I noticed several men checking me out. I gave them my best mysterious smile. Not too much, I had to appear aloof and fetching. I stared ahead, sucking my cheeks in a little to appear more serious and It-girl-like. My peripheral vision confirmed that despite my right-from-the-gym look, I was definitely the center of attention. My new sultry, pain-free self was intoxicating!

Transaction completed, I felt the heat of hungry eyes following me from the teller window to the door, and was on top of the world.

Next on the itinerary: the post office. As the clerk ran my credit card for the book of stamps, I glanced behind me to find several wayward eyes on me again. All hail the fleece vixen!

By the time I got to the grocery store, I was practically sashaying like a runway model. Who knew that getting my back fixed would catapult me into the beauty equivalent of moving up to the next tax bracket?!

I got home and brought my purchases inside. My husband was sitting at the dining room table and I gave him a drive-by kiss on the way through to the kitchen.

"What's the white thing sticking out of your shirt?" he inquired.

"Oh, that's just the label," I answered smoothly, referring to the large tag sewn onto the outside of the sweatshirt.

"No, Romi, I mean the thing hanging down like a cape," he persisted.

I glanced over my shoulder to find a stark white pillowcase that had been tucked into the back of my sweatpants by my thoughtful therapist to protect my clothing from the massage gel, hanging out of my shirt down to the backs of my knees.

I laughed so hard no sound came out. My husband just shook his head and rolled his eyes. "My wife, ladies and gentlemen," he said.

"OH MY GOD!!!! Do you have any idea where I've been?!?" I finally shrieked hysterically. I regaled him of my morning's adventures and he started laughing too.

I think we both knew in that moment we would never see a white pillowcase the same way again. I also knew that in quiet back offices all over town, the security personnel digging each other in the ribs as they replayed the tapes wouldn't either.

BATH TIME

As the credits rolled up on the movie du jour, I announced the impending bath time. Mia leapt up and grabbed my hand. We walked hand in hand up the stairs, pausing randomly for her to peek through the slats at my husband, who was sitting on the couch downstairs.

"I see you, Daddy!" Mia chirped, pressing her little face into the space between the stairs.

"I see you, Mia," came the response, and he ran over to press his face into the space from the other side of the stairwell. Mia shrieked with laughter and we advanced one stair.

"I SEE YOU DADDY!!" she bellowed, and we repeated this little ritual until we got to the top of the stairs.

At the landing, Mia took off and ran into her bedroom.

"Let's get a washcloth," I called after her, and went into the bathroom to start filling the bathtub.

Two seconds later, I heard the pit-pat-pit-pat of her feet as she came scurrying into the bathroom, wielding a washcloth that was pinched between her forefinger and thumb. She held it up in front of her like a contaminated medical waste disposal kit. I reached for it but she dropped it a moment shy and it fell on the floor. I scooped it up and hung it on the towel rack.

Mia was ready, her bath crayons in hand. She was flitting around in her pre-bath dance mode, and I finally cornered her so that we could take her clothes off and get this show on the road. She was too preoccupied by the crayons to notice that I had taken her shorts off. Score one for Mommy: this occurred without any protest.

"Right arm," I said, and started to help her out of her right sleeve. She wriggled away and was halfway up on the toilet by the time I grabbed for her again. "Mia, right arm, pumpkin," I reminded her and we got the first arm out. I pulled her to me before she could squirm away again and we repeated this process for the left arm. I peeled her T-shirt up over her head just enough so that it was out of her eyes but still trailing down her back like a turquoise veil.

Her eyes lit up and she smiled from ear to ear. "I want to see in the miww!" she exclaimed.

I picked her up and plopped her in front of the mirror over the sink. I held her steady and she leaned forward until her face was inches away from the glass. "I'm gonna have a baff," she informed her reflection.

"C'mon, love, time to get in." I carried her over to

the bathtub.

"Color a big shark!" she commanded, thrusting the blue crayon in my face.

"You color for now, love," I told her.

My little Matisse got going, announcing each step as she brandished her crayons with bold, broad gashes and furious dots.

"She's eyes," Mia said, scrawling in wide circles. "She's tail," as the blob got a stylized line through it.

I immediately got to the task at hand, working swiftly with the washcloth, following her back and forth as she strode about the tub. I took full advantage of the distraction and moved when she moved: when her arm went up to put the stripes on the zebra, I got in quickly and washed under her arms. When she lifted her head to scout for the next rendering site, I dove in under her chin.

A tiny piece of lint floated past Mia's left leg. Even though she was deep in concentration, this intruder did not escape her peripheral vision. "Mommeeeeeee!" she yelped, leaping away from it and flattening herself against the back wall of the tub. "Take the fuzzy away!!"

"Oh Mia, it's just a piece of nothing," I said nonchalantly, "It's probably from one of your socks."

"Mommy, take the nothing away!" was the perturbed response. I fished around while she attempted to scale the bathtub wall and extricated the offending piece of microscopic cotton.

"You not gonna wash my hair," she cautioned

sternly, her eyebrows bunched up in concern.

"Actually, I *am* going to wash your hair tonight, love," I burst her bubble.

She was instantly panicked. The crayon fell, immediately forgotten, as she lunged into my shirt and grabbed fistfuls of the fabric into her white-knuckled hands. Somehow after two and a half years, this was still a terrible ordeal for her each and every time. And her despair gnawed at this mother's heart a little more each night while we went through it. "I'm just going to wet your hair, sweetheart, why don't you look up to the sky and then it won't go in your eyes?" I suggested.

She had no regard for my idea and started bopping up and down, wailing. I poured the first cup of water on her head and as the volume of her crying intensified, I wondered if the neighbors thought I might be dipping her in battery acid.

While she will eventually come to appreciate this, much to her current chagrin, Mia's hair is so thick that it takes several cups for water to even penetrate her mane. She had now stretched the neck of my shirt into a slack sack and was clawing at my throat. I had to gently push her back as she had buried her head so far into my chest that I couldn't get the shampoo onto it. She was bawling and I tried to reassure her.

"It's okay, love, let's put the shampoo on your head just like the monkey," I tried, referring to the picture of the monkey on her shampoo bottle. Technically, he's not really getting his hair washed, but she thought the green bushy leaves behind his head were soapy bubbles and I left the reference intact, needing all the help I could get.

I lathered her hair and attempted to massage her scalp, but again, ran into some trouble accomplishing this task as she continued to press her head into my chest.

"Right, sweetheart, close your eyes and keep your face up," I prepared her. Sobbing. The first cup of water rolled down the back of her neck and she leaned her head forward.

"Look up to the ceiling." Nothing. "Look up at Mommy's face, love," I coaxed. More howling. There was now a foot on my stomach and she was reaching around my neck to pull herself out of the tub.

"Mia!" I unwrapped her limbs and put her back into the tub. "I have to get the shampoo out of your hair!"

"NooooOOOOOOOO!!!!!!!" She was frantic now. At this point, I just needed to rip this proverbial band aid off so I dumped the water over her head and rinsed the soap out as quickly as I could. The poor girl was spluttering and weeping and clutching me so tightly that I almost toppled over into the bath with her as she thrashed wildly in the water.

"All done!" I trilled, and try to wipe the drops, tears, soap and terror off her face with the washcloth. Her eyebrows were red in indignation and she had the look of a feral cat that had just been captured. "See? That wasn't so bad?!" In the same way I imagine spending an hour in a cage of rabid dogs wouldn't be so bad either.

"I want to come out," Mia begged pitifully, and I

hugged her into a big, fluffy towel. She clung to my neck and put her sodden head on my shoulder.

I hugged her even more tightly and kissed her flushed cheek. I rubbed her back and tried to dry her, but there wasn't much point to this exercise as I believed there was more water on my drenched shirt than in any of the reservoirs in the northern hemisphere.

I thought wryly about the picture on the box when we bought Mia's infant tub: a grinning, happy little boy, relaxing amid the bubbles while his adoring, hired-for-the-shoot Mom looked on. Who are these children?! Was there truly such a thing as a good bathing experience?? Or was this just- as I strongly suspected to be the more realistic scenario- a clever scheme made up by the marketing people to get clueless parents like me to buy the bath?

Then I saw the reflection in the mirror. My little munchkin was all smiles and dimples and her spiraled hair looked as fresh and delicious as it smelled. I caught my own face. It was love and patience and the face of a mom who, despite the daily performance of an epic Greek tragedy, wouldn't trade in her little character for all the water babies in the world.

CRABBY CABBIE

This time I had been diligent. Contrary to my typical method of flinging items into the suitcase 42 minutes prior to leaving for the airport, this time I had actually packed the night before, a time that was usually reserved for some frantic laundering of the said items. I'd even called and booked the cab a few days prior to the departure date, as my husband was working late and wasn't going to be able to take me to the airport.

Six thirty was the arrival time I had requested of my transportation service, and even more contradictory to standard behavior, I was ready to go at six.

Which was just as well.

At about three minutes past six, the phone rang. I leapt off my perch and ran to answer it.

"AAAHLAAAAAHFGEKASDAAAEKLFLKJKL SIIIIAAAAAJHGKOOAJSFK!!!!!!" shrieked the voice on the other end of the line.

"Um …pardon?" I ventured. This was not the time for prank calls.

"KAHFINELAKDJALKEJROOOOOKSJHSFJH AAAAGKUAAJFHGKJGH!!!!!!!!" he continued? Repeated?

Now mind you, I am the person who has been forwarded voicemails from people at work to "translate" the shattered English of poor foreigners who had the audacity to leave their messages with their accents lilting to varying degrees of comprehensibility. Having gone through the process myself, I have a soft spot for anyone else who has left their homeland for the greener pastures of emigration. Admittedly, I had the advantage of English as my first language when I moved to the United States, but am always baffled by subtitles during news interviews with people who are clearly speaking my native tongue albeit with a dialect of some kind.

Sensing that this frantic outburst had something to do with the cab that was supposed to be at my apartment within the next half an hour, I struggled through the database in my head to find the source of this strange, seal-like barking.

Alas, I couldn't even place the planet, never mind the nation, of origin of this man, which rendered me totally mute.

"I'm sorry, I don't understand you, please can you repeat that?" I eventually inquired, which was really a ridiculous question, as his repeating his statement seventeen times would not have helped in this particular case.

I believe I only angered the man even more as he

promptly hung up.

I called the number for the cab company and explained to the dispatcher that I had just spoken with a very angry man who I believed to be the driver, and that I thought he must have been lost. I confirmed the address again, and let them know that I would go to the front of the apartment complex and wait for the gentleman so that he didn't have to twist around the sometimes confusing maze of little roadways within the community.

Par for the course, it was pelting with rain when I stepped outside. Dragging my suitcase behind me, I trudged through the sop and got to the front of the development. I took shelter under a carport and waited for the cab to arrive.

After about ten more minutes, a green van pulled into the driveway and stopped about four inches from my nose. I ran around to open the door, but the cab driver was already there. He took my suitcase and quickly loaded it into the back of the van. In a flash, he was back around the passenger's side of the car and opened the front door for me.

We both climbed in out of the rain and slammed our doors shut.

"Hi," I smiled, turning to face him.

"HOW YOU NOT KNOW WHERE YOU LIVE?!?!?!?!?" He roared at me.

My eyes must have looked like saucers and I felt my mouth drop open a little. I blinked a few times, but was at a total loss. I just stared at him.

"You say Stevens *Street*!! It's Stevens ROAD!!!!!"
He was gesticulating wildly at the street name sign.

I came back from my temporary out of body experience and recovered with, "They all say Stevens, it's one long street that winds around."

"NO, NO!!" He insisted, "It's Stevens ROAD!!!!! See??" We were still in park, and he was now thumbing through a very well used and outdated Thomas Guide. He pressed the map into my face and said, "See? Stevens ROAD! There only one Stevens in the book!"

Hmm, I dared ponder (exclusively inside my own head of course), perhaps I'm going out on a limb here, but that might possibly be the right Stevens then?

I was starting to get irritated but, wanting to keep the peace, offered an apology and turned my head to stare at the buckets of rain beading off the freshly waxed window. He started the engine and away we went.

"I can't understand, people not know where they live," he kept mumbling. "How you not know?"

I glanced over and saw him shaking his head like a horizontal bobblehead doll, sighing sharply with little eruptions of air like the bursts of steam escaping from a pressure cooker. The air in the cab was humid despite the vanilla-scented air conditioning that was blasting on my knees. I listened to him berate me for several more minutes as if I was a disobedient student acting up during after school detention.

We got to the corner right before the freeway entrance and stopped at the red light. I seriously considered telling him to shove it and getting out, but I had to be at the airport by 7:30 and couldn't chance not getting replacement transportation in time.

So I relaxed and figured it was an adventure if nothing else.

We were seven minutes into the journey. There was a brief respite of quiet and then he just couldn't help himself.

"Jesus Christ!' he hissed under his breath, shaking his head anew.

The humor and absurdity of the situation hit me like the hail on the roof. I craned my face even further to the right so that he wouldn't see me grinning from ear to ear, and struggled to get the better of it for a minute or two before I could let my neck snap back around.

Now I was really curious. Just how long was he going to stay angry about this? I waited until we were on the freeway to speak.

"Do you have to pick up anyone else?" I gambled, trying to make conversation. Maybe now he was late to pick up other passengers.

"No, you last person of the night," he answered. I clamped down on another smile. We coasted to a crawl in the 205 Friday night rush hour.

"I'm sorry you have to drive around in such bad weather," I commented. "And in this traffic too!"

"Oh, no problem," he gave me a huge grin, "I love driving people."

I couldn't hold it any more. The laughter fell out of my mouth and he eased up too. By the time we got to the airport, I had heard most of his life story and was delivered at the shuttle drop-off point a few minutes ahead of schedule.

He leapt out of the car again and presented me with my bag. I thanked and paid him and he slipped something into my hand as he passed me the handle.

His business card.

"Let me know the next time you need ride!" he bellowed jovially, and waved goodbye like an old friend as he climbed back into the green machine and sped off into the torrential night.

HOW WOULD YOU LIKE YOUR CASH BACK, SIR?

Before my working career led me to the corporate side of employment, a world where I would discover pleasant, air-conditioned environments awash with trinkets emblazoned with the company logo, I paid my dues in some less noteworthy roles. One particular stint, however, stood out among the rest.

Spending one more college summer as a bank teller was going to be the death of me. The people I worked with were really sweet, but if I had to justify to one more angry businessman with $600 to his name who had been banking there since before I was born why I couldn't let him withdraw $595 of it without his identification, I was really going to lose it.

I decided to try my luck in LA instead, where I could spend the summer hanging out with my boyfriend and best friend while we hunted for the perfect seasonal job.

The first few weeks were spent in optimistic freedom while she and I cruised around and scoured the newspapers, putting in applications everywhere we could. But three weeks into it we were at the bottom of the draft pick barrel and needed to get hired, fast.

In desperation, we conceded to a promising-looking ad for a maid service. We figured we could work together, and really, how difficult would it be to clean houses for a few months?

We found the address and pulled up next to a building whose windows were festooned with a quaint combination of polka dotted bullet holes and graffiti. In our nineteen-year old naïveté we thought nothing of it and went inside.

We were greeted by a large, relatively empty room, with a desk at one end and a long table at the other. Both pieces of furniture looked like they were purchased at a used and then used again office furniture store.

There were dented metal chairs lining the walls and dingy, moth-eaten carpet that was peeling itself off the floor in a protracted attempt to escape.

We approached the man sitting at the desk and let him know we were there to fill out applications. He eyed us a little leerily and gave us each a double sided application. He let us know we could use the table to complete them and gave both of us a pen.

We seated ourselves between a voluptuous, split-end-haired blonde whose fake boobs looked like deployed airbags bursting out of her tank top, and a kind-looking elderly woman with orthotic shoes. The four of us were lost in studious concentration, filling the pages with our impeccable references and most compelling reasons for wanting to scrub toilets. The silence was broken by Inga the Swedish bikini model, who was drumming her inch-long hot pink acrylics on the table top.

"I used to clean houses naked," she offered, her gum popping from somewhere inside the cherry Wet n Wild glossed mouth. "All the husbands would stay home. It's amazing, I used to make so much in tips!" she continued in fascinated awe.

I knew I couldn't look at my friend as it would all be over if I did. We bowed our heads down a little lower and I could tell she was biting her lip as hard as I was biting mine. I glanced sideways at the elderly lady and found she was completely still, as if in suspended animation, her eyebrows knitted together in deep contemplation. I couldn't help looking at her application which was completely blank except for the words "I love cleand."

The next adventure took us to the local movie theatre.

"I'd hire you right now but I think you're over-qualified," said the manager dubiously.

"No problem!" we cried in unison, "We really don't mind." The perks included watching free movies and as we were dean's list college students, this job should be a snap.

He shrugged and handed us our uniforms. We were to return in a week to start, and become the newest additions on the payroll.

On the first day of work, I stood in the lobby in my black polyester outfit with bright turquoise and purple accents that was a foot and a half too long, and white t-shirt underneath as instructed, waiting for my training to begin.

The manager who had hired me was nowhere to be found. I was loitering outside one of the theatres when the doors flung open under the surge of a stampeding herd of adolescents who tromped past me like a tribe of refugees who had just been set free. One of my contemporaries was waiting in disillusioned patience on the other side of the doors. As the crowd starting thinning out, he thrust a broom in my hand and said, "Clean number two."

"What *is* number two?" I shot back, irritated. He motioned to the just-vacated theatre and I tentatively followed him into the darkness. Between us we swept up two industrial sized rolling garbage cans of opaque popcorn remnants, masticated globs of gum with teeth marks still in them, soggy soda cups and sticky candy wrappers. I felt a piece of my innocence die as I crawled on my hands and knees to reach some kernels on the floor that were in crevices the broom could not reach.

"Let's go!" yelled the uninspired veteran, "There's another show starting and we have to open the doors back up."

I gathered up the few shreds of dignity I still had left and went towards the shockingly bright lights of the lobby.

My next assignment: the concession stand. I was shown to the left side of the counter. It was the opening weekend of Apollo Thirteen and the popcorn machines were broken. To appease the unhappy patrons, huge bags of pre-popped popcorn were brought in and were propped up against the wall, ready for the swarm. It was 112 degrees and the air conditioner had decided it was a perfect time to go on strike as well.

Class was over. I was now an Employee, with all the rights and responsibilities thereof. The throngs descended upon the counter demanding their snacks. I discovered that the "butter" machine was nothing but a crude oil pump and was panicked that my own arteries were clogging by association as I dispensed partially hydrogenated heart attacks onto the troughs of popcorn. There was a slick layer of oily sludge on the floor and I had to move about in a mock skating motion so as to avoid slipping in it.

The candy was kept in neat, enticing stacks in the glass display case. The Junior Mints were a hot item in my line and quickly flew off the shelves. I had just vended the final box when I heard a small voice ask for more. No problem, I would just ask the folks at the other cash register to loan me a few temporarily until the rush was over and we could restock.

"I can't give you any of mine," clipped one of my chubby colleagues. Her hair was pulled up into a knotted ponytail in the center of the top of her head that was so tight it was pulling her eyes up like a bad facelift. "These are for this cash register and we can't switch sides."

Switch sides?? I wasn't trying to defect, I just needed a box of candy!

I glared at this self-righteous girl and struggled with the urge to kick her in the head. "There are people in line who want them and I don't have any. You do. I NEED THE CANDY!" I hissed at her and skiied over to grab them myself. She put her hands on her hips and squared her body to me, glaring back with a raised, overly-plucked eyebrow that let me know no good would come of this. Dear God, I begged, please don't let me die over a box of Junior Mints.

He must have heard me as my belligerent peer was pulled away from the counter to make a hotdog from the greasy wrack of bratwursts that had been leisurely rolling up and down the pan longer than I'd been an employee.

The stagnant heat combined with the lubricated air was causing my hair to cling to my dewy face. From across the lobby I saw a friend of my mom's and ducked under the counter, pretending to look for something until she went into the theatre.

Salvation! It was break time and I glided out of the alligator pit to go to the break room.

"Hi! I'm Chuck!" I was instantaneously greeted as soon as I poked my head around the door. Chuck's glasses were thick with big, round plastic frames and he had a smile from ear to ear. He was sitting at the table, finishing his coke.

"I'm Romi," I said unenthusiastically.

Chuck grilled me for a while on who I was, where I was from and what I was doing in LA. I explained that I was a college student who was basically trying to make enough beer money for the next year at school.

"Wow, you're like, an adult and everything!" he exclaimed in revered wonder.

I smiled weakly and tried to pick up and read the newspaper but in incessant intervals of two minutes or less, Chuck persisted in interrupting.

"You should come over and hang out with my friends. We would have a blast. What do you say?"

Fifty seconds later. "My birthday's August 7th. We're going to get a bunch of beer and party at my brother's house! You should totally come over."

I wasn't sure where this was going so I thanked Chuck for his very sweet offer and gently broke it him that I was pretty seriously involved with someone.

Chuck was unfazed. "That's cool! He can come too!"

I thought all was quiet until a piece of scrap paper slid under the newspaper. On it was scrawled a phone number and reminder that I should call if I was available on the 7th. From my friend Chuck. I still have it in my scrapbook.

The infernal night drudged on until it was time to close. The sweat had created a landscape of tiny streams that crossed each other all the way down my back until they conjoined in a soaking puddle of moisture at the base of my polyester shirt which had miraculously not managed to absorb a drop.

My final task of my first day: to clean the disgusting, undulating sausage machine that still sizzled at a temperature more severe than the seventh layer of hell. For half an hour, I wiped that thing until I could hear the sound of a forest crying, mourning for one of their own that had been sacrificed to produce the mountain of paper towels that were necessary to accomplish this mission.

The perspiration was dripping into my eyelashes and I stood back, trying to blink away the salt as it bored into my corneas. Freedom was only minutes away. Once everyone else finished the last of their closing routines, we would lock up and go home.

Like the descriptions of astral travelers being snapped back into their bodies only inches from the light, so I was led back to the wiener churner by a gigantic man with shoulders as big as a bookcase and a large, round shiny head.

"You're not going anywhere. This needs to be clean," he demanded in a voice that sounded like an idling motorbike.

"I did clean it!" I protested shakily to the very unjolly giant.

"Well clean it again!" he boomed and thundered off.

I scrubbed the filth, again, until whatever fingerprints the first cleaning hadn't seared off did so now, and the gargantuan hulk was satisfied with my attempt.

I called my boyfriend to pick me up and waited the

twenty minutes on the sidewalk, curled up in an upright fetal position. I saw his car pull into the parking space and I flung open the door like there was a swarm of bees chasing after me. My boyfriend had tuned into the fact that I was moments away from a meltdown, so he graciously didn't press for details.

When we got home, however, his father took one look at me and burst out laughing. I, in turn, started sobbing.

I walked past them and went straight into the bathroom where, still crying, I turned on the tap in the bath. As I lay in the tub sniffling, I daydreamed about my next college summer at home. The one where I couldn't wait to ask, "How would you like your cash back, Sir?"

ZOO

We'd dawdled so long that we left at 10:30 in the morning, and I knew it was crazy to even attempt it. It was going to be a seventy degree April day, an almost unheard of jackpot after months of unrelenting rain and hail. Like all the other Northwesterners, we would be outside, voraciously slurping up the sun's rays like addicts.

I had run through my mental go-to list of places that would hold Mia's interest while allowing me to try and coax some dormant melanin out of hibernation. I had casually mentioned the zoo to her the night before, and as anyone with a small child knows, that is a legal, binding contract. We were going to the zoo.

Unfortunately, so was everyone else who claimed a child under the age of ten on their taxes. We rounded the corner and the stream of cars was backed up to the employee entrance, a place we usually sail past on our way to the gate. The stupidity of this decision sat on my head like a dunce cap but I had promised my little girl that we would go to the zoo, and by God, here we were!

We merged into the line of cars oozing into the parking lot. Contending for parking spaces should be a competitive sport. It brings out an unparalleled selfishness in people. Moms, dads, grandparents and older siblings who I suspect to be ordinarily courteous people pulled out right in front of us in an aggressive attempt to claim their spot, and I in turn, cut others off too. We circled the parking lots like buzzards waiting for a doomed deer to take its last breath. The Parking Fairy, always so loyal, was not coming through for me today. In fairness, I couldn't take it personally; she was just spread too thin.

It dawned on me that even if we did find a spot, the zoo would be teeming with hot, frustrated little children, jostling my timid daughter out of the way as they jockeyed for coveted positions in front of the railings, and crying over spilt ice cream and sleeping animals who weren't available for viewing after the wait to see them. The thought added claustrophobia to the bubbling cauldron of impatience that was threatening to ignite my shrinking fuse.

Half an hour went by. I pulled over, resigned to the fact that we would just have to wait it out, and began to deeply resent humanity in general. It occurred to me that we might spend these precious hours of glorious sunlight in the car, waiting for some yahoo who just happened to park in the spot where I was hovering to finally get tired and take his clan home. Another five minutes went by. Three spaces behind me a family appeared like a mirage and opened the doors to their car. Before I could even blink, the driver of a van that had just come up from the entrance flicked on his turn signal and marked his territory.

Something primal inside me snapped. I could not waste another solitary ray of sun. "Love, I don't think we're going to find a parking spot," I said.

"Yeah, all the cars are in the way!" she agreed.

"Should we go see the boats instead and come back to the zoo another day?" I ventured.

"No, I want to go to the zoo," protested Mia softly.

"But sweetheart, I don't think we'll be able to get a parking space," I tried to break it to her as gently as possible. I turned in my seat to face her and looked guiltily into her wide, green-brown eyes. "We might just sit in the car for a few hours and then have to go home for our nap," I continued. "Or, we can go and see the boats and go for a walk," I finished hopefully, wondering if she'd bite.

I felt like a total heel. Wouldn't any self-respecting parent have waited for a spot if it killed them so that their offspring could have their day?

"Okay, Mommy, let's go see the boats," Mia agreed good-naturedly. "Maybe later we can go to the zoo."

I was completely humbled. Most children would have thrown a huge fit or at least shed a fair amount of tears at the prospect of changing course like this, especially in the parking lot, so close that we could practically smell the dusty dung at the bottom of the exhibits. But here she was, my three year old, exhibiting more grace than I have seen from people many years *my* senior.

"I am so proud of you, Mia!" I exclaimed. "Thank you for being so good about it and not crying! You are such a good girl!" I cooed. She grinned and my heart ballooned with love and admiration for her. I would have put the car in park and jumped in the back to give her a hug but the person behind me was riding my bumper with a grim look that told me he was advancing forward whether I was going to do so or not.

We broke free of the steel pack and headed further east on the freeway. Within minutes we were at the harbor, having had our pick of parking spots, with the river sparkling in the sunshine and the gleaming white yachts bobbing on the rippling water. It was perfect.

We went for a walk, Mia bouncing along in her pink t-shirt, grey leggings and pink ballet tutu, and me strolling behind her. I breathed utter satisfaction and felt my tension dissolve as we walked past the restaurants and shops.

"I'm hungry, Mommy," Mia piped up, with impeccable timing. We were outside a coffee shop.

"How about a muffin?" I offered.

"Ooh, I love muffins! That would be very tasty!" She concurred. We sat down at a wooden table and shared a muffin, with freshly squeezed orange juice for Mia and coffee for me.

Tummies full, we continued our meandering. Dodging the landmines of goose poo, we tiptoed across the lawn where a young boy was nearly airborne as his huge kite swooped up and down through the air. We gingerly made our way down the rocks to the water's edge and watched the geese swimming leisurely in the gentle waves that lapped at the sand.

Mia, who has an irresistible urge to pick up all bits that nature has expelled, ran along the bead-like pebbles collecting as much as her little hands could hold. When we clamored back up the rocks to the walkway, her inventory included two pieces of woody, reed-like sticks, a feather, a twig, a diamond-shaped, fleshy leaf and a few crushed dandelions that she had been clutching since we left the coffee shop.

Next we ventured down the gangplank to the quay where the boats were moored. We walked to the end, taking in the dragon boats along the way. Their brightly painted heads nodded to us from the undulating wakes of several yachts that had just sailed.

On the way back we stopped by another patch of weeds for my daughter to ransack their tiny white flowers. She sat down to pick off the miniscule petals so I plopped down next to her. There was a deliciously mild breeze coming off the river and it danced with the coppery highlights in Mia's hair.

I wanted to drive back to the zoo and thank each person who wouldn't yield their space to me. While Mia loves the animals, there is always a power struggle between her and I as I try and teach her to let other kids have a turn, or when she doesn't want to see the monkeys even though the other mom and kids who we went there with do, or when the roar of the confounded animatronic T-Rex freaks her out and she practically climbs up onto my head in terror and won't come down.

This tranquil day at the harbor was effortless. It was one of those quiet reminders that you are in the right place at the right time, and that all is as it should be.

Long before I was pregnant with Mia, I had a vision of myself standing at the ocean with a little girl. She was about the age Mia is now, and had dark brown ponytails, with deep chocolate eyes and dimples in her chubby cheeks. I had watched her jumping in the water.

While the narcissistic fantasy version of my daughter bears only a slight resemblance to the real live miniature of my husband's face, I had somehow tapped into her spirit, because the little girl right here at the river with me was exactly who I hoped my daughter would be. And again, while not the ocean scene my dramatic mind had conjured up, here was the moment, the picturesque day at the water with her.

To think, we were only one minivan away from missing it.

UNINVITED HOUSE GUEST

At a decidedly ungodly hour on a Saturday morning, I was awakened by a deepening smell so foul it made my eyes tear and my nose and mouth burn.

I immediately identified the stench of the union between burning rubber and a week-old pile of unwashed jockstraps to be the work of a skunk. After the initial assault on my shattered olfactory nerves, it came through the vent above the bed in swelling waves like an acrid crescendo.

I threw back the sullied warmth of my duvet and stomped into the bathroom. The odor was unbearable and I instinctively held up my shirt sleeve in front of my nose. Unfortunately it was coated in skunk as well and only served as a more potent reminder of why I wasn't still asleep.

Grabbing the spray can of air freshener from under the bathroom sink, I strode downstairs, my finger squeezing the trigger the whole way down. I circled the living room and kitchen leisurely while the can hissed a steady dose of antidote into the poisoned air. However, this feeble attempt was no match for the efforts of the intruder and I gagged on the new combination of rubber-jockstrap-fresh linen.

I heard footsteps other than my own, and found my husband standing beside me in his own rumpled state. He flicked on the light outside the kitchen window to reveal the two offenders: racing-striped furballs with their tails up in the air, chasing each other around our patio.

I am not a violent person. I believe all creatures have a right to their lives and try to see the good in everything and everyone. But I now found myself fantasizing about flinging the whole drawerful of sharp knives out the window in the hopes that a few of them will see to it that these reeking trespassers were brought to justice.

They scurried out of the light and, my husband suspected, under the patio. I whipped out a notepad and started googling numbers for the Humane Society and Washington County Animal Control. My husband mentioned that there are pellets made from fox urine that ward off skunks as they don't like the smell. The irony of this was not lost on us: Outstinking the stinky?? But I was willing to spread rhinoceros crap on the lawn with my toothbrush if there was a chance it might help. He seemed to think the hardware stores would carry it so I jotted down the numbers for Lowes and Home Depot as well.

We went back upstairs and attempted to go back to

sleep. My poor husband had to get up in an hour to go to work and I had plans to take my daughter ice skating with some friends around noon. Eventually the sandman wrestled the scent to the ground long enough for us both to drift into a merciful slumber.

In the shower later that morning, I washed my hair three times, bathed with soap and then scrubbed my skin almost raw with tangerine sugar scrub, hoping the oils from the scrub would mask the eau de putrid on my body. I was tempted to stand in the frigid bathroom and drip dry, as I was sure my towel was laced as well. A slathering of cocoa butter lotion came next, followed by a splash of perfume. The heating came on and shoved another round of rancid oxygen up my nostrils. It was so vile I had the urge to jump back in the shower and wash, rinse, repeat, wash, rinse, repeat until my soap and shampoo were all used up.

My brother, who was staying with us for the weekend, had noticed a smell but didn't think it was too terribly bad. I typically operate under the assumption that smoking is a nasty habit, but was now cottoning on to an obvious benefit and wondered how long it would take the nicotine to kill my sense of smell too? I toyed with the idea of asking him to smoke inside the house for a nice breath of fresh air.

With all the windows open, I started on my list. The county line was more involved with dogs and cats, but did offer the number for an animal control service. I called and got Suzanne, a woman who listened sympathetically as I impressed upon her the fact that I could not wake up one more morning by way of the skunk alarm clock. She explained that this was mating season and sprays increased this time of year as the females' way of telling the males no. Couldn't a simple "not tonight honey I have a headache" suffice?! She took my name and address and we set up the appointment for Monday at noon.

Right before we were ready to hang up she said, "Hold on, where are you?" I gave her my cross streets and she replied, "I'm in your area, I can come over now if you like?"

I was too choked up with gratitude to even speak. "Oh…my…God," I finally whispered reverently, "Thank you."

Suzanne chuckled and told me she would be there in ten minutes. I'm not sure if she said anything else after that because I couldn't hear her voice over the deafening chorus of angels singing "aaaaaaaaaaaah" in beautiful, divine harmony.

Suzanne showed up on schedule and went about inspecting the house. My husband and I were willing to take out a second mortgage if needed but her rate was exceptionally reasonable and covered thirty days of service. She set out two traps and showed me how to open them if a stray cat should get stuck in there while we waited for the amorous couple. She also showed me where the dig marks were on either side of the porch where these blasted gatecrashers have been hiding out.

I learned there is such a thing as a type of animal retaining wall that goes a foot deep and six inches across under the patio that would help us avoid becoming the number one vacation resort of the rodent world again in the future.

I hoped Suzanne would get a commission for this should we have it installed. Hocking my heirloom engagement ring would be a small price to pay to make sure I am never awakened by the smell of skunk gland again.

We got to the skating rink and I felt like a walking garbage can. I apologized to my friends who kindly insisted they couldn't tell Mia and I smelled like we'd been brawling in a diaper genie. However, as the afternoon wore on, the scent of animal rejection emanating from my bag became so repulsive that when we eventually went to lunch in the food court, even my credit card was rank when I fished it out to pay for our meals.

We all managed through lunch and as we climbed into the car, Mia clutched my arm and informed me she had to poo. I attempted to negotiate a trip to the bathroom but she smiled her most heartbreakingly adorable smile and said politely, "No thank you." A mere formality, I asked again if she'd like to go to the potty. I knew asking her again is like finding nothing in your closet to wear and then looking again five minutes later in the hopes of seeing something new, but I figured it was worth the futile try.

"No thank you," she confirmed, and promptly squeezed my forearm a little harder. I knew the deed was done. Knowing my daughter is mortally afraid of public restrooms and since the horse was already out of the gate, I decided to change her in the car. It was only after I artfully shimmied the training pants down over her ankles that I realized I had no bag in which to dispose of the soiled bundle. Beaten, I packaged it as best I could and placed it on a large piece of paper I found on the floor of the car. The hand sanitizer provided a brief respite of refreshing lemon before it dissipated into the thick air.

As we hurtled down I5 towards home, I turned on the fan on the dash and enjoyed the pleasant whiff of exhaust fumes all the way home.

THE WEEKDAY WALTZ

Though it killed me to wake her up, I couldn't let my daughter sleep any longer.

Each morning I walk the fine line between letting my daughter soak up as much of the last, precious minutes of sleep as possible, and leaving enough time to give a very opinionated preschooler enough time to quibble over everything so that I get her to daycare, and ultimately myself to work, on time.

I quietly opened the door to Mia's room and padded softly across the carpet to her bed. She was curled up against the mesh guardrail; a cherubic, fleecy angel, with one pink sock on her left foot, the other on her right hand, and an army of stuffed animals littered across the bed.

Her ribs gently rose and fell with her calm, even breath, and her mouth was open ever so slightly.

I reached out and tenderly smoothed a hand over her back. "Time to wake up, pumpkin." My voice was almost inaudible, but I knew the successful execution of the next half hour's activities hinged on releasing my child from the sandman's clutches as gently as possible.

She cracked open an eyelid and squinted at me leerily. "I was crying in my bed," she declared piteously.

"You were?" I sympathized. "What's the matter?"

"You didn't come and get me!" she scolded.

"Mia, I did come and get you, I've just woken you up and I'm here aren't I?" I reasoned with her.

"I'm not going to school today," she announced, changing the subject as she always does when the argument isn't tipping in her favor.

"Sweetheart, you know you have to go to school today. Do you want to get changed on the bed or on the floor?"

Her shoulders slumped forward and she plopped down dramatically onto the bed, folding her legs and arms like a little pretzel. Although her head was down, bottom lip curled ever so slightly in a shadow of a pout, she looked up at me through the chestnut coils of hair and her big greenish brown eyes were pools of gloom.

While her act of defiance had derailed us already, I secretly found this whole exchange very amusing and asked her again. "Bed or floor? I'm going to count to three and then I'm going to choose. One…"

The "w" sound was barely out my mouth and she was already scrambling out of the bed. She came to stand next to me and sighed a long, exasperated sigh. "Fine…" she muttered, head still down, the very picture of dejectedness.

I pulled two shirts out of the drawer. "The purple

one or the kitty cat?" Her eyes darted back and forth, weighing her options. I saw the smile get the better of her.

"The kitty cat," she grinned.

Point: Mommy.

I tossed the shirt onto the bed. "How about the pink pants?" I suggested, taking them off the shelf. Although the pink pants matched nicely with the kitty cat shirt, my motive was not so much to prepare my child for a future on the runways in Milan as it was to get the haggling process underway.

As expected, she balked at the offer and strode over to the dresser. Clothes began spewing from the shelf like a fabric volcano as she rummaged through the neatly folded piles to find the outfit du jour, flinging them over her shoulder as they failed her inspection. "I want to wear a skirt," she finally concluded, producing a turquoise ruffled skirt with large, white hibiscus flowers on it.

"That's fine," I said, "But it's cold out and you have to wear tights under it." I saw her nose start to wrinkle. "That's not negotiable!" I intercepted.

Mia sighed another long-suffering sigh and went wordlessly to the sock drawer. For all the rebuttals she has thrown at me over the years (and they have been numerous, and laboriously debated), for some reason the phrase "not negotiable" has struck a chord with her and so far, always gets her to back down. I'm not sure if it's the words themselves, or the tone in which they are delivered that makes them so effective. All I know is, they work. Consistently. Thus I use them judiciously so as not to diminish their power, so that when I need it, this ace up my sleeve is the perfect antidote to the incessant challenging of my authority.

She scrubbled around in the drawer, and again, miniature pairs of socks, tights and underwear went flying in all directions. She pulled out a pair of brown tights with large pink, purple and red circles on them, and the look of pure satisfaction on her face told me she needed to look no further.

While I'm sure the designers at Versace would be appalled at this ensemble, Mia's choice of outfits is not a battle I'm willing to fight. We have been to the supermarket in princess dresses with muddy rain boots sticking out the bottom, and various places with her "bra" – the stretched out loop of fabric formerly serving as the band to keep my hair out of the way when I'm washing my face - on the outside of her shirt. In my opinion, as long as she is warmly clad when the weather is cold, how she does it is her business.

She put her selections on the bed and stood there motionless, her head hung low.

"Come on, love, let's get your jammies off." I had to keep things moving along.

"I'm a sack of potatoes," she answered glumly. "I can't even move."

"Oh NO!" I exclaimed in mock horror. I rushed over there and lifted up her left arm. She provided no resistance, so I let it fall and it plummeted into a swan dive and hit her thigh with a dramatic slap. I saw a flicker of a smile dance across her face. "We better check the other one!" I said, and repeated the exercise with the right arm. Whap. Another little smile. Her eyes were sparkling.

"It's not working!" she bleated. "I'm still sacky!!"

"Then there's only one thing left to do," I said in a serious tone, and began tickling her mercilessly. Within seconds she was howling with laughter and that broke the ice. Her PJs went sailing up into the air, and I tried in vain to catch and corral them.

Finally, she was dressed.

Her room looked like a children's clothing store had thrown up in there, but that too was something I was not going to deal with at this point in the day.

I walked out onto the landing and started down the stairs with my right arm extended, hand open. Within seconds I felt Mia's little hand clasp onto mine and we walked downstairs in perfect harmony, like two debutants entering the ballroom.

While every once in a purple moon my child is actually in a cooperative mood when she wakes up, I assume she will be in rare form every morning as she is today. So I have learned to get everything prepared before I even venture into her room. Waiting patiently for the conclusion of this morning's performance of *The Neglected Girl Who Was Actually A Sack of Potatoes* was my lunch bag, Mia's cup of dry cereal, her cup of milk, my handbag, both of our jackets, my laptop in its bag, her shoes, my heels, her umbrella, my umbrella and my car keys.

It was only after the birth of my second child that it occurred to me to go one step further and actually put all this stuff into the car before I went to wake the kids, but I digress.

"Mia, please bring me your hairbrush," I said. She flitted over to the bathroom. I realized I had forgotten my travel canister of coffee and went to grab it. I emerged from the kitchen to find her sprawled on the carpet, drawing a picture on her notepad. "Mia, where's your brush?" I inquired.

"I'm drawing, Mom!" she retorted.

"Love, we need to leave right now or I'm going to be late and then I'll get into trouble," I told her. Technically, I'm exempt, so I'm not really going to get into trouble, but getting into trouble is a consequence to dawdling that my daughter can conceptualize at her tender age.

"Will you get a time out?!" she gasped. To Mia, this is the ultimate punishment. I have never even had to administer this chastisement; the mere threat of it has been enough to keep my daughter in check thus far.

"Maybe," I said gravely, hoping it would spur her into action. Mission accomplished, she leapt up and ran into the bathroom. Seconds later she sprinted back out and popped the brush into my hand like a baton in the relay race. I felt a little bad for putting this one on her, but sometimes as a mother it just comes to this.

Hair brushed, we went to sit on the bottom stair to put on our shoes. Mia had picked up her cereal, and began to grunt and pant while she tried to shove her feet into the sneakers without undoing the Velcro or putting the cup down.

"Take the strap off first,' I instructed, and scooped up the myriad of items and headed to the garage door. As I put my finger on the button to open the door, I heard a frantic yell.

"MOMMEEEEEEEEE!!!! DON'T LEAVE WITHOUT ME!!!!!" Mia was running to the door, stumbling over her half-fastened shoes in her haste to get to me. She tripped over one of my shoes and her Cheerios went flying all over the floor.

"Sweetheart, I'm not going anywhere without you," I reminded her. "I was just going to put this stuff in the car." She exhaled and relaxed a little. "Let's pick up the Cheerios," I sighed.

"Okay Mom," she agreed jovially.

We picked up what we could, and I threw them into the trash. I poured another cupful of the little Os into her container and we headed back out to the car.

"Let's have some tunes!" Mia said as we backed out of the garage. I turned the radio on and away we went. "Mom, you know, when you look at the sun, you're looking at outer space!" She chirped.

"That's true," I affirmed, "but you must never look directly at the sun, love. Do you know why?"

"No," she said.

"You can fry your eyes, just like an egg!" I said.

"That's right!" she agreed. "And then you would have to peel them to see afterwards."

"No love," I corrected her. "Once you fry your eyes

you can never un-fry them. That's why it's so important that you never look at the sun."

My daughter nodded and turned her attention to the window. A few minutes of silence elapsed while she chewed on that piece of information. Soon we were nearing the turnoff for the street that led to the little red school house.

"Mom," Mia began, "Do dead people go to the bathroom?" I was caught a little off guard by this question as I was not in the least bit prepared to respond to inquiries about the deceased and their methods of personal waste disposal. So I turned the tables on her. "What do you think?"

She gave this another smidgeon of thought. "I don't think so. Otherwise they would get to heaven and say, how did I pee my pants?!"

I felt a huge grin widen my face. "That's a good point," I agreed.

We found our parking spot right out front. Mia scrambled out of her seat and out onto the sidewalk, and skipped to the door, her hair bouncing wildly as hopped from leg to leg. I signed her in and she immediately became quiet, adhering tightly to my left leg.

"Good morning Mia!" smiled the teacher at the front desk. Mia said nothing, and stared at her through lowered lids.

"Good morning," I responded, and the teacher and I smiled at each other. This was the daily ritual; despite the fact that Mia had been going to this daycare center since she was three months old, she still became sullen at drop off time.

I shuffled to the classroom with Mia still wrapped around my leg, and dragged her through the door. I knelt down and gave her the biggest, tightest hug I could without crushing her. When I pulled away, her head was so low her chin was touching her chest.

"Sweetheart, I love you and I'll be back for you this afternoon," I said. Mia didn't budge. Even my most heartfelt assurances never seem to ease her fear.

"Mia," I said, lifting her chin, and found her eyes swollen with huge tears that were teetering on the edge of her lids. She was genuinely fighting to hold them back, and this quiet courageous struggle is what gets to me each morning.

"I don't want you to go," she whispered, her face crumpling a little with the effort of trying not to cry. "Please don't leave me."

Now I felt the tears prickling my own eyes. The grand scale theatrics are one thing but this was real, and we both knew that I had to leave her.

"I love you pumpkin," I repeated, and hugged her again. She squeezed me back, and I heard a little sniffle in my ear. "Have a wonderful day, I'll see you later on, and I can't wait to hear all about the fun things you'll do today!" I said brightly. She didn't buy it, and with her head still buried in my neck, squeezed even harder. I started to stand and the teacher, who had been watching this farewell, stepped in.

"Come with me, Mia," she said, putting her hands

around my daughter and literally peeling her off me, "Would you like to help me take note of everyone who's here?" Mia shook her head and resisted, and the teacher pulled harder. I advanced toward the door, and Mia was still clinging to me, the space between us growing as the teacher got a better hold of her.

Then we were separated, and I blew Mia a kiss and winked at her as I started walking out into the hallway.

"Have a good day," the teacher smiled.

"You too," I replied. And I turned and walked away with my parting gift: the image of my daughter giving in to her tears, her soulful, despairing eyes scrunched as she stood in the doorway, softly weeping.

I sat down at my desk and put my laptop in the docking station. As my computer booted up for the day, I put on my headset and dialed the number and then the passcode. Do-do-do-doop-do-do. I was now connected to the call. The familiar voiceover lady on the prerecorded instruction began her welcome blurb. I cut her off and pressed the star key, then my host key, then the pound key. The lady let me know that she was joining me to the conference, and the call commenced.

"Hi this is Romi," I began, as I stared at Mia's latest school picture pinned to the cube wall right above my laptop screen, "Who do we have on the line?"

MR AND MRS JOLLY GREEN BUY A COUCH

I was not going to dignify that with a response. I didn't even bother to slow my stride. "Romi!" he called out again, "You *have* to come and sit on this one!"

A few seconds later as I was almost out of earshot: "Romi!!"

I stopped and sighed, my back still to him, and felt my eyes do a little fluttery roll. I just knew which couch he was talking about, it had to be the fawn colored, L-shaped monstrosity that was occupying most of the sales floor.

A slow pivot confirmed my suspicions. My husband was seated on a piece of furniture that looked like what might have happened if a bag of marshmallows and a recliner had had a baby and fed it steroids for breakfast. It was the quintessential man couch, equipped with flip up foot rests, a place for the remote, and of course, cup holders. And it was approximately the size of a tour bus.

After eight years of marriage, our recently expanded family combined with the falling apart of our very generously handed down couches dictated the need for a new place to sit. Like many couples, my husband and I struggle with the gentle tension between our differing opinions about form and function. However, we have an extra layer to contend with- my husband is 6'4" and I stand about sixteen inches shorter than him at a glorious 5'0".

Needless to say, our sense of scale is a bit dissimilar and finding a couch to simultaneously fit legs like telephone poles and upside down bowling pins was proving to be quite a tall order. Not surprisingly, our recent shopping expeditions had failed miserably in this pursuit.

My husband's face had the expression of a little boy who was asking if he could keep the stray puppy he'd just brought home. Thus, despite myself, I loped over to my join my mate at the beast, formulating my plan on the way over. I would plop down on it for a moment to appease him and then gently burst his bubble.

"Its microfiber!" he exclaimed gleefully as I approached, "Just feel it!"

I suppressed another eye roll and placed a reluctant hand on the armrest. My fingertips were instantly pampered by the fluffiest fabric I have ever felt. It was as if someone had upholstered this marshmacliner with a leviathan teddy bear, and I begrudgingly had to concede that point. I shot my husband a look from under my raised left eyebrow.

"Yes, it *is* very soft," I began, "but…"

"See?" he broke in, "Sit down! You have to sit on this thing."

"Love," I tried again, "it's just too big! Not only would I need a stepladder to get on and off it, I don't think it would fit in our living room." I don't think it would fit in City Hall.

"It's perfect!" he countered. His long limbs unfolded across the pillows in ideal proportion to their gargantuan prop.

"Come on, just sit down," he coaxed. In order to speed this up and be on our way, I backed up to the built-in chaise longue on the end of the right-hand side and eased myself up and onto the gigantic cushion.

Oh no. No, no, no, no, oh… no.

I was now officially in a terrible quandary. My whole body sank into the padding like chocolate into a mold. There was no denying it: this was hands down the most comfortable seating apparatus my weary bones had ever had the fortune to grace. Yet it was the largest (not to mention ugliest) thing this side of Jack's beanstalk.

Was I prepared to come to terms with this monster truck of the settee world, where perching upon it would mean my feet could never touch the ground? How would we actually get this thing into the house without having to take the roof off first? How was I ever going to find the impetus to peel myself off it?

My husband sensed my weakening resolve and went in for the kill like a spider whose fly has just been mummified in its web. "You know, if we got it, we could sell our bed and just sleep on this!" he taunted. While I knew he was joking, I was about to break it to him that this wouldn't be an issue as they would be delivering the couch sometime soon with me still blissfully sprawled on the chaise.

Just then the salesman arrived. "Can I help you folks with something?" he smiled down at me. It was a knowing smile; he had seen my kind before and knew he just had to reel me in.

"Grhrmmmmhhhrrrr," I gurgled back, unable to move, unabashedly reveling in the luxurious cushiness.

"Comfy, isn't it?" he took the next step.

"Mhhrf," I agreed.

He and my husband discussed pricing and measurements while I remained at one with the behemoth for a while longer.

Eventually, using every ounce of willpower I could muster, I heaved myself off the couch, feeling like I'd just had a massage, won the lottery and got twelve hours of uninterrupted sleep.

"We'll call you," I slurred at the salesman. "We just have to make sure this will fit."

On the way home, my husband and I ran through all the pros and cons of this potential purchase. It was huge. And the most comfortable couch we'd ever sat on. And huge. And microfiber, which was apparently easy to clean. And enormous.

While I was visibly relieved when we ran out of measuring tape in the living room and indeed, found the couch would have pretty much run from wall to wall, part of me was admittedly a little sorry to say goodbye to the dream of owning the most comfortable specimen I'd sat on yet and probably ever would again.

We did finally find our compromise, as we always do. Like the very definition of the word, our new seating arrangement strikes a nice middle ground between our divergent needs and body types. The added bonus is I don't even have to get a running start to get onto it.

A PROBABLE VIRUS

I was sitting cross-legged on the kitchen floor with my daughter, squeezing out a play dough worm when the pain started.

Out of the blue, the ankle that was pressed against the floor was intensely sore. I shifted my weight onto my hands to change position and stretch out my legs, and my back, calves, shins, fingers and wrists also cried out.

It was so sudden and so severe that the only logical explanation was that I had obviously been abducted by aliens, who had pulled out my internal organs, bones and muscles, pounded them for several hours with a steel mallet, stuffed the whole lot back into my skin with a boxing glove, and then transported me back in a time machine.

I popped a Motrin and resolved to complete the blue dinosaur I was being challenged to make.

The next day at work, I was surprised to still need

pills to get through the morning. My generous pain tolerance is luckily inversely balanced to my complete lack thereof for drugs, so a miniscule dose of anything usually sees me through without a problem.

But it was barely taking the edge off.

I writhed through several meetings trying to get comfortable, but with every atom of my body feeling bruised there would be no finding chair-side nirvana.

The other indication that something was amiss was my marked lack of appetite. I am the person who only felt mildly disinterested in food during the throes of appendicitis, a time when most folks are practicing for the projectile Olympics.

The day after that, with the physical assault easing up, I skipped my newfound habit of narcotic Skittles and noticed the 102.7 degree fever they had been masking. I have never had a fever above 101 in my life so the inferno in my eyes and cheeks was a new experience.

I finally called the doctor when, five days later, I was still cooking at 103 with chills that chattered my teeth so hard I thought they would shatter.

They took blood and noticed my white blood cells were low. The strep test came back negative. With no other symptoms, my mysterious illness was diagnosed as a probable virus. I was given a prescription for antibiotics to ward off any other potential pathogens, as my waning white blood cells would be fairly ineffective at combating anything else that might come along while I got over the nameless virus. I was sent home with the understanding that if any other symptoms showed up, to call back and make another appointment.

Five days after that, the 103 fever broiled on and I grew an ostrich egg between my left ear and jaw line. In a mid-afternoon meeting at work, I casually smoothed my hand along the right side of my neck, and came across what felt like a string of peas all the way down into my collar bone.

The fever packed its bags and vacated the premises but not before leaving me a souvenir: a repulsive white spot on the back of my throat. The tonsil underneath it swelled gloriously, as if to showcase the diamond lodged inside it. My tongue decided to join the party and expanded until its edges were scalloped from filling into the tiny spaces between my teeth. Speaking from these crowded chops became more and more difficult and I sounded like I was smuggling a pound of hot coals in my mouth.

Several more trips to the doctor revealed nothing until online research showed me the light. I called the doctor and demanded a mono test.

"The test takes about five minutes," he said and asked some questions to pass the time. He checked after two minutes to make sure it was working and the case was already solved.

"I'm sorry, mono is horrible," he said sympathetically. The kicker is that there is nothing you can do about it. A virus, mononucleosis just has to run its course and all you can do to facilitate healing is sleep and drink lots of fluids. I strongly suspected the recovery wouldn't be quite as bad if I was smashed through it, but apparently alcohol did not count as fluid in this case.

The doctor kindly started writing a prescription for heavy-duty knocker-outers. For a split second I entertained the idea of taking and filling the script, I figured the chunk I would get for them on the black market might help cover my medical copayments. However, I realized I wouldn't even be in the position to negotiate such sales for quite some time and informed him that vicodin, percoset and darvoset just made me throw up. He put his pen down.

What ensued was total agony relieved only by respites of blissful sleep when I finally passed out from exhaustion. My other tonsil got an invitation to the ball and went in costume, dressed as a cantaloupe. I ate extra strength Tylenol like popcorn. I wondered if my insurance company would cover one of those saliva suction machines like they use at the dentist, and then considered paying full price for it anyway, if it meant I would never have to swallow again.

One night I woke up gagging violently. I shot up in bed gasping for breath, trying to exorcize the sandbag that had lodged in my throat. It took me a minute to realize I was choking on my own uvula.

My bewildered toddler was having a hard time making sense of her new tough love regimen.

"I can't pick you up, pumpkin," I said, when she held her arms up to me at the top of the stairs. My arms, previously endowed with standard-issue, superhuman mommy strength, were now as effective as spaghetti that had been forgotten in tepid water for a few hours. My back, previously akin to that of an ox, felt as sturdy as a house of cards.

Her little face was concerned and she pondered the situation for a moment. Then she lit up. "Can I kiss it?" she offered, and leaned in to plant several tender kisses on the small of my useless spine. "Now you can pick me up!" she tried again triumphantly.

I smiled as my heart dissolved at her sweet attempt and wished fervently that her earnest gesture could have done the trick.

"Sweetheart, unfortunately I am going to be sick for a while," I broke it to her as gently as I could. After several days, she burst out crying. My husband and I discovered she thought I was mad at her because I wouldn't pick her up or kangaroo hop around with her. That hurt worse than the mono.

Having survived for three weeks eating only over the counter drugs, gatorade and apple sauce, I ventured onto the scale, just for kicks. What I saw was in violation of the laws of nature. According to my digital scale, I was still hefting around the same amount of flab I'd had prior to the onset of this fun fest. "THAT'S NOT POSSIBLE!" I barked garbledly at the miserable piece of glass and metal. I turned away in disgust, incredulous that even my scantest of caloric regimens had failed to make the numbers budge so much as an ounce.

When I got to the point that I literally couldn't talk,

I threw in the towel. I emailed my boss and requested a week off work.

"Make the bed and don't clean anything. I'm coming next week," announced my mom over the phone. I could have cried for joy but couldn't risk the tears causing anything on or around my head to swell even a smidge.

She dropped everything to fly 3,000 miles and spent a week as maid, babysitter, chauffeur, cook and laundromat. As guilty as I felt, I permitted myself the much appreciated help and gave in to the fatigue. My days and nights blended together in a patchy, netherworldly existence.

While my mom shuttled my daughter to and from daycare, fed and bathed her and got her to bed, and my husband toiled away the erratic hours at his retail occupation, I slumbered like a newborn.

Like the tentative rainbow emerging at the end of a battering storm, the shards of glass in my throat subsided and I found I could emerge from my cocoon for a few hours at a time. My mom dropped Mia off at daycare and we actually managed to go out for lunch together. I felt like I'd just been paroled.

Six days after she'd arrived, my (Fairy God)mother left, leaving behind a clean house, happy granddaughter and enough meals in the freezer to keep the American Red Cross in business with at least two third world countries.

Despite my vengeful scale, I could tell by the unearthing of my cheekbones and sagging waistline of my jeans that I must have lost *something*. I furtively stepped back on the vile weighing device to press my luck and found that sure enough, seven pounds had melted off during my unconscious hiatus.

Was it wrong that I was elated? No, I rationalized, one has to look for the silver lining. I felt like one of those infomercial success stories: with a nasty case of mono and only about four weeks, those pounds will just lose themselves! I did it, and you can too!

The recuperation was long. I'd heard from friends that it drags on and you feel like you're never going to get better. They were right. For months afterwards, if I went to bed any later than eight o'clock I would pay for it the next day with exhaustion so crippling I would feel physically ill.

But time heals all wounds, even the ones brought on by mono.

"You can pick me up today!" cheered Mia as I hoisted her effortlessly into my arms. It was exactly three months after my unwanted guest had reared its monstrous head, and we were on our way out the door.

"Yes, baby," I agreed, smiling at her. "Yes I can."

CORPORATE GHOSTS

We were called to an end of day meeting in the President's office. I had been expecting this day for many months so I already knew what they were going to tell me.

My fellow manager sat to my left. Next to him, the Manager of HR, and to her left, the President. His hands shook slightly as he dialed the call-in number and we waited for the Ops VPs to join on the line.

They gave us the "it's not you, it's us" speech, which I must admit I found mildly amusing: My company was breaking up with me and they used the same clichés as awkward teenagers.

The hourglass had been tipped upside down and I could feel the sand start to run. My team was given six months until our last day. I wondered how many other thousands of laid off Americans were also walking the halls as corporate ghosts, caught between their unfinished duties as they trained their replacements, and the promise of the new possibilities that lay waiting once their badges were surrendered to HR on their final day of employment.

The reality of the word "disposable" became clear to me at this time. While we know that no-one is indispensable, each of us believes that we are special. That when the time comes, even though our position has been eliminated, the company would recognize in us something extraordinary and want to retain that quality in their midst.

But the truth is, while nothing personal, to the corporate machine I was simply an added expense, and I am as ordinary and replaceable as the next person. I understood then that eight years of staying late to finish projects, coaching others, coming in late on Sundays to test systems, doing volunteer work, and a virtual mountain of accumulated knowledge was not enough. That there was nothing I offered that was so unique it would save me from the axe.

And I knew that despite those eight years of servitude, my memory will fade. At first, folks will tsk and say, "Romi would know the answer to that!" And every so often something might trigger a joke about "remember when Romi used to..." But as the weeks melt into months which yield to years, the next wave of veterans will ask, "Romi who?" And I will disappear into a vaporous remnant of this company's past, a coat of color that once changed the walls but has long since been painted over.

As they went over the logistics of the project plan that was going to turn me into a new statistic in the unemployment rate, I couldn't help feel a sense of relief. After bumping into the elephant in the room for months, I could now look at it head on.

No stranger to saying goodbye, I have been through the grief of the end and how it brings a whole new beginning.

So I vowed to myself that while I was still there, I would put my all into giving the last bit of myself. And I will be even stronger for the next incarnation. Wherever that may be.

HOOPTIE DO

No-one ever *intends* to drive a hooptie. Just as no four year old dreams of being "mediocre" or "average" when they grow up, driving an outdated, gently dented jalopy is not something one particularly *aspires* to; it is simply something that just happens to some of us, for one reason or another.

I am one of those individuals whose driving history has been punctuated with a respectable vehicle here and there in amongst the rattletraps. In glancing back at my life, I realize driving a disgrace on four wheels is not only my prerogative, it's my birthright.

My earliest memories of childhood include a bright orange Citroen my parents affectionately dubbed the Pumpkin. The chocolate brown interior served as both a complement to the Halloween orange paint job and satisfaction of the mandatory '70's color palette, and it held a hallowed spot in our driveway for many moons.

All any child of a hooptie-driving parent wants is to disappear into thin air as quickly and quietly as possible so as to attract as little attention to oneself when your friends or, perish the thought, your crush of the week is in the immediate vicinity. My mother, a soul far too practical to take these trifling notions into consideration, genuinely had no inkling of the embarrassment factor when she took ownership of this car, which had an intricate hydraulic suspension that had to "rise" like a loaf of bread while I died a thousand deaths in the back seat waiting for this blessed event to occur.

Compounding the issue was the method in which my mother chose to alert me to her presence when she came to pick me up. While the other mothers pulled up in their sleek BMWs and Mercedes coupes and sedately gave a honk or two, my mom would whip around the corner in the Pumpkin with her signature PAARP PARP-PARP-PARP-PARP PAARP PAAAAAAARP!!!

When I wasn't being delivered to or retrieved from places in Cinderella's post-midnight coach, my grandparents would get roped into taking me to birthday parties or school functions. I then discovered true mortification lay in being dropped off outside a group of the cool kids in a twenty year old Valiant that was as long as a city block with an interior that included furry, bright aqua seat covers.

My prayers were finally answered when my poor unsuspecting grandparents' Valiant was stolen in plain daylight. The cute little Honda they bought to replace it timed perfectly with my approaching middle school.

When I turned sixteen my parents shared their Chrysler Fifth Avenue with me, a car that I despised with as much passion as it loathed me in return. After several close calls, at the age of seventeen I fell asleep at the wheel of this monster on 71 South after dropping my boyfriend at the airport in Columbus. I did several doughnuts across the freeway before depositing the miserable hunk of metal in a muddy ditch on the side of the road, thereby neatly breaking its front axle.

Then there was my first car. A gift from my aunt and uncle who were basically junking it after it had made the rounds through their three children, it was a very generous and sweet gesture and I appreciated the fact that I had a car to call my own. This vehicle had been a Buick once upon a time but the U and K had fallen off, leaving us no choice but to call it the "BIC."

The BIC was a light, golden-tawny color, which is the first indication that a car is destined for Hooptie-hood. Incidentally, as you may now have ascertained for yourself, the fact that a car is given a name other than the one its manufacturer bestowed upon it at the factory is a definite second sign. Having the ignition, air conditioning and radio on at the same time caused the BIC to stall, so being seventeen I opted to sacrifice the air and roll down the windows in the suffocating Midwest humidity.

The BIC eventually developed a peculiar habit of stalling when it came to a complete stop, so I had to drive it like a stick shift even though it was an automatic and slam it from reverse into drive while it was still rolling. When approaching a red light, I had to keep one foot on the gas, revving the engine slightly while I braked to prevent it from cutting out. This necessitated a delicate bit of choreography once the light turned green, beginning with a roar of the engine and puff of smoke when I took my foot off the brake and squeezed the gas pedal a bit harder. This was usually followed by a healthy backfire as it lunged forward, and concluded with all cars on the road around me lagging further and further behind until I was driving in a sputtering bubble of solitude.

There was the grey Sundance in college, another very sweet hand-me-down, from my grandfather this time, into which I poured the equivalent of several reservoirs worth of oil, almost as quickly as it leaked out the bottom.

The Tercel met a sad end. The first non-beater to which I had a set of keys, it was totaled the week before my wedding by a crazy man in a minivan who was driving illegally in the section of the road where cars are usually parked, in a residential zone. He barreled into me at sixty miles an hour as I was turning into a side street.

After the wedding, when we were a step away from living under a bridge and eating cat food, my husband and I marched in and out of nine dealerships, looking for the salesman who was willing to give us our deal: two thousand dollars down and payments of $150 per month. We weren't playing hardball; it was literally all we could afford.

Naturally, the only car at the Chevy dealership that finally fit the bill was the four door Prizm with a steering wheel, four tires and precious little else. The sticker touted the tint as "sand" but it was your basic, standard-issue hooptie brown, and my friends christened this one "the Poo."

As of this writing, the Poo is paid for, and has a relatively conservative 82,000 miles to show for its eleven years of service. It did suffer a rather fierce keying several weeks after we first brought it home that took the finish off down to the metal. While the auto body shop tried gallantly to buff out and paint over the etchings after the car was subsequently sideswiped, Ian's ardent feelings for Kayla are immortalized on the hood. The seals around the window frames are chipping and peeling off and it has kissed a pole or two in its day.

The CRV is the first non-hooptie car that I purchased new, with power windows and locks, a sun and moon roof, volume control for the radio on the steering wheel and one of those thick, remote-entry keys that makes the satisfying whoop whoop noise when you lock the door. This is the car for which my husband and I compromise: whoever has our daughter for the day gets the CRV, while the solo driver has to cruise around town in the Poo.

Driving a clunker makes one the Rodney Dangerfield of the road. There is simply no respect for those whose automobiles squeak, stammer, shudder, wheeze or growl.

However, I finally realize what my parents, grandparents and apparently many other operators of the decrepit sedan underground know too: A car is just a car, to get you from point A to point B. Sure, it would be nice to have a car that turns heads in a *good* way, but I came to comprehend the world isn't going to go careening off into outer space because I'm not driving the latest Lexus.

That sort of reasoning, I also realize, is why I will be the source of excruciating embarrassment for my own daughter when I sail up to a parking space in my heap de jour, watching her slink lower in the seat until she is practically climbing out of her skin trying to stay under the car window so the boys don't see her.

I have also come to understand that eventually, by virtue of the fact that I inhale air and have two eyes, I will embarrass my daughter beyond recognition. Hence, does it really matter if that humiliation stems from the car or from something equally as egregious such as me talking to her in public or liking certain music?

Instead we will choose to keep the Poo for as long as it runs or until someone runs into it, and maybe use the money we would have spent on car payments for a fabulous vacation. A break from reality where we will rent a gorgeous convertible, perhaps one with a bumper sticker that reads "My other car is a hooptie."

BOILED SOCKS

I consider myself to be someone with a fairly diverse palate. Not sophisticated necessarily, just open to new eating experiences, undeterred by textures, and equipped with an "I'll try (almost) anything once" attitude. I say almost, because I do have my boundaries.

However, there are so few of them I can name the list off the top of my head: internal organs such as kidneys and liver et al, and anything that belongs in a cliché fairy-tale recipe, i.e. blood and eyeballs, snails and chicken feet. Since all those items are lumped together in my book as a lower class culinary level along the lines of in-an-emergency-and-stranded-on-some-gorgeous-but-remote-island-and-have-exhausted-all-the-fish-but-not-quite-resorted-to-sampling-the-cockroaches-break-glass-and-eat, I don't consider them to actually be food anyway.

But there is one more item on my list of the woefully unpalatable. This offending offering is a sinister side dish in that at first glance, appears to be an ordinary, unassuming vegetable. Yet once the cooking process begins, these little green balls release a malodorous, underhanded powerhouse of stench that smells to me like boiled sweaty gym socks. Brussels sprouts.

Try as I might over the years, I have never, ever warmed up to this sneaky skunk of the leafy green world. As a child I would turn up my nose when they appeared on the menu for dinner. My mom told me they were baby lettuces, an idea that did endear them to me enough to pop one in my mouth, only to be greeted somewhere between the table and my lips by that special smell that is theirs alone, before forcing a few down my gullet. As far as I'm concerned, they taste as bad as they smell.

Once out there on my own, I ignored Brussels sprouts. It was my prerogative and was a perk of my newfound independence. I am an avid lover of all other vegetables and never felt the void of avoiding this one.

But as I matured, every once in a while I would meander back to test the waters, just to see if they were really as bad as I remembered. I tried them steamed, barely boiled, fresh and frozen. And indeed, they delivered on their pungent promise every time.

I was finally about to write them off for good when my daughter asked if we could try them for dinner. I couldn't remember whether it was a federal offense or a deadly sin to tell a child she can't try a new vegetable, but I wasn't going to risk violating either one. I needed a plan and a friend at work offered a suggestion.

"Roast them!" she said.

I was still skeptical but she insisted that when roasted with some herbs, they were really good and nothing like the gaseous stink bombs to which I was accustomed.

So I decided to give it one very last shot. A grown woman, I was willing to do this dance one more time and then, if they were still the revolting methane spheres they kept proving themselves to be, I was going to walk away with a genuinely clear conscience and never look back.

I handpicked the little sprouts myself. They were very fresh and hit the color wheel at a vibrant, healthy shade like just-mowed grass. I pushed my prejudice aside and tried not to sneer as I tossed them with a little olive oil, garlic, salt and pepper. Dubious to say the least, I tucked the pan into the oven and kept a scornful eye on them as I turned them over a few times.

Dinner time arrived and with it, the chance to put the theory to the test. Incredulously there was no compost heapish aroma as I brought the fork to my hesitant tongue. There was a *slight* hint of the familiar stench when I actually bit through, but all in all, the verdict was distinctly mild compared to my previous experience. Naturally this might have been attributed largely to the spices and olive oil as opposed to the actual sprout but nevertheless, I was prepared to concede this one graciously.

My daughter, however, didn't have to say anything. The shar pei-like wrinkles on her nose and look of horror in her eyes were fairly telling.

While nothing that will be accompanying my entrees on a regular basis, I do have to admit the roasted version has successfully changed my perception of Brussels sprouts. Until this night, I had viewed them as one of those "love it or hate its" like sushi or roller coasters. There are some things in life that are unequivocally good or bad, fun or boring, yum or yuck. However, there also exists a plane where things subsist in the more forgiving and interesting cracks in between these extremes. So, it appears this one will need to move off my list of what to serve for dinner when Satan perfects that triple axel.

My stance on bone marrow, however, has not budged one iota.

NIGHTMARE

It started with a tiny whimper but as is the case with all mommies, jolted me urgently from my slumber at three in the morning.

I craned my ear to the monitor, hoping my daughter was just talking in her sleep, as is so often the case. A few seconds of silence and then another whimper. I flicked on the camera and she was still lying down, her eyes closed.

Maybe she was just crying a little in her sleep, something that also happens from time to time. I plopped my head down on the pillow and waited with bated breath to see if she would settle down, or if this would ultimately require my intervention.

About ten seconds elapsed and I heard more whimpers, these a little louder and closer together. They began to intensify and took on a soft, even, sobbing sound.

I turned the sound down on the monitor and threw off the comforter. As a child, I was plagued by nightmares too, and still remember the terror and need to have my mom's comforting hug to make them go away.

I opened the door quietly, hoping that maybe we could salvage this one yet, that she would go back to sleep and in turn, so would I.

I padded over to the bed with my stealthiest footsteps, and she whipped her head up as soon as I got near. She was turned around, her feet resting on her pillow and her head facing the foot of the bed. In the dim glow of the night light I could see her curls were matted to her forehead and her cheeks were flushed.

"What's the matter, sweetheart?" I cooed as I scooped her up into my arms. She was very warm and still smelled like sleep.

She was totally discombobulated and looked around the room erratically, blinking. "I had a bad dream. I'm done sleeping," she garbled, rubbing her eyes with her little fists.

"Um, no sweetheart, it's three in the morning," I said. "Look how dark it is outside." I took her over to the window and pulled back a few slats of the blinds.

Her face crumpled and she started crying again. She buried her muggy forehead in my neck and wept. "It's okay," I reassured her while I rubbed her back, "Mommy's here and I'm going to come and lie in your bed with you for a little while." She tightened her grip around my neck.

"I'm hungry, Mommy," she sniveled.

"Let's go get a little snack and we'll bring it up

here," I acquiesced.

"Thank you Mommy," she smiled, so instantly gratified that it made me smile too. We bumbled down the stairs and into the kitchen and I put a few goldfish crackers into a cup for her.

Back upstairs, we crawled into her bed. She sat up, concentrating on her cup of crackers. I focused on clearing a path so I could have a square inch on which to lie down. Her elephant, a large, brown monkey and several, smaller stuffed animals were relocated and I fluffed a pillow for myself next to hers.

"I'm all done, Mommy," she said, absently handing me her cup. I put the empty cup on the chair next to her bed. She was happy and content, as if the fierce interruption to her sleep had never happened.

"Okay, pumpkin, now it's time to lie down and close our eyes," I said. I lay down and pulled one of her blankets up over me as far it would reach without uncovering my toes.

"Okay Mommy," she gleefully agreed and lay down next to me, our heads inches from each other. I felt her damp ringlets next to my ear.

"Goodnight my sweetheart," I soothed, and kissed her cheeks and forehead, "Sleep well."

Ten seconds went by.

"I love you, Mommy," she said and popped up to look at me.

"I love you too, sweetheart, go to sleep," I said, gently helping her back onto her pillow.

Two seconds of quiet were followed by copious

flapping, her arms and legs in the air, negotiating her comforter.

"What are you doing?" I asked.

"I'm putting on my mermaid!" she exclaimed, with an air of surprise, as if she couldn't imagine I didn't know what she was doing.

"There will be plenty of time to be a mermaid tomorrow," I said, "lie down and close your eyes."

"Okay, Mommy," she concurred. I half-heard the next half hour or so of chatter as I dozed in and out of consciousness.

"No more talking, sweetheart, it's time to go to sleep," I heard myself mumble.

Another minute or so of silence was broken. "I love you with my whole heart, Mommy."

"I love you with my whole heart too, Mia," I smiled. She was so sincere and tender. "Goodnight sweetheart." I closed my eyes.

"Mom?" came a little stage whisper. I chose to ignore it as I knew this could go on until the sun came up. A beat. "Mom," she breathed again. I kept my resolve.

Even with my eyes closed, I could sense her head inch in closer to mine, until I felt her breath against my nose.

"Mom." It was a little more audible, a mix of whisper and sound.

I opened one eye. "Yes, Mia?"

"I love you so much with my whole heart, Mom!"

I couldn't stifle the chuckle, and kissed her juicy

cheeks.

"Goodnight, I love you with my whole heart too."

I closed my eyes again and was almost out.

"Mom?" came the hushed tones again. Again, I ignored her attempts and pretended to be asleep, hoping she'd follow suit.

"Moh-mmy," she whispered in a sing-song. A little finger forced my eyelid open.

I sat up. I had intended to stay until she nipped off but it was obvious that she just wasn't going to go to sleep while I was there. "Right, sweetheart, I'm going back to bed, let me tuck you in." I climbed out of her bed.

Her brows furrowed. "NO, Mommy!!" She started to fake cry, little forced noises that I knew were just for show.

"Mia, you don't have to pretend to cry, it's time to go to sleep, I love you, sweet dreams," I wrapped it up as I planted another kiss on her head.

I headed back to my room. A glance at the clock confirmed that we had lost an hour of sleep. But, despite the circumstances that had brought us together, I felt good that I could be there for her, that I was able to chase the proverbial monsters away. I realized the magic of parenthood is revealed to each parent as needed, like an unending elixir ready to be tapped at a moment's notice.

I knew I would be tired at work the next day but it didn't matter. I had made my daughter feel safe, just as my mom had done for me. And I figured an hour was a pretty small price to pay for something this important that money can't buy.

SAMOOSA

The theme of the potluck was South Africa. The usual staples were already nabbed: bobotie, boeries and melk tert. I was given the freedom to choose my dish, and being the stellar planner that I am, emailed my brother and his girlfriend the day before to find out if they needed an entrée-ish item, i.e. cottage pie, or desserty contribution, i.e. brandy tart.

The answer, retrieved on my iPhone the following day- aka about 6 hours to go and counting - was that it was really up to me but perhaps a side dish would be most welcome.

I thumbed back through my aunt's South African cookbook and it became increasingly clear to me that I was going to make samoosas. These savory Malaysian pastries, filled with vegetables such as potatoes, peas and onions and seasoned with a plethora of exotic Eastern spices, are a foundation of South African cuisine. As a child I remember buying these scrumptious crunchy triangles from street vendors on the weekends. They were hot and fresh and the crispy dough was a perfect complement to the soft, steamy vegetables contained within.

Mind you, I have never made samoosas.

Also bear in mind that I am the poster child for culinary mediocrity. While my cooking has proved to stave off basic hunger and not yet caused any fatalities, I will not be responsible for Emeril Legasse's sleepless nights in the foreseeable future. Despite the fact that my past is peppered with middle school home economics electives and after school cooking classes, until recently I generally didn't embark on any gastronomic adventure that didn't begin with "open the box" or "pour the cereal into the bowl."

However, given that I was virtually raised on these delicacies, the instinct to make them would surely kick in, much like how teeny turtles just know to make their way to the water after they hatch.

Another compelling reason to attempt these goodies from scratch was the sting of a recent baking botch-up. This past Christmas I showed up to a cookie exchange with my bag of bakery-bought items only to find that everyone else had not only been up until the wee hours baking their homemade confections and pastries but had thoughtfully arranged them on festive platters.

On that day I learned that the thought is not always what counts: sometimes one simply has to break out the rolling pin. (Provided one can actually locate it in one's kitchen.)

Boiling the potatoes and chopping the vegetables

went swimmingly. I even managed to make the dough, from scratch, and got it to the point where I'd wrapped it and set it aside to rest for half an hour.

The simmering of ingredients in the pan and measuring out of all the spices was equally routine; however, I became vaguely aware that the kitchen was starting to look more and more like a compost heap, with carrot and potato peels strewn about and bits of chilis and onions littering the sink and countertops.

While I waited for the filling to cool, I turned my attention back to the dough. Wrapped in wax paper, it had turned to a gluey, sticky ball which instantly adhered to the rolling pin like epoxy. I tried to extricate the lumpy mass from the rolling pin, but instead succeeded in transferring it onto my hands where it stuck like a globulous mitt. My husband stepped in to the rescue and spooned some flour onto the board, where I wrestled with the dough until it finally surrendered and fell off the rolling pin.

"Paper thin" was the exact specification as to the required thickness of the dough. I knew my manilla flubber was not going to permit me to get it paper thin and I grunted as I attempted to half-roll, half-beat it into submission. I finally got it to the thickness of a generous tortilla and called it good. I cut the well-floured dough into the 3" x 10" strips as directed and laid them across a plate.

Mia was hopping around, waiting with a spoon in her hand to help me. "Okay, ready?" I smiled cheerily at her.

"Yes, Mom!" she responded, bounding over to the counter.

"Let's wash our hands really well before we start," I coached.

"Why?" she questioned.

"Because we want to make sure our hands are clean so that there are no germs on the food," I explained. We scrubbed and dried our hands like a pair of surgeons prepping for an op.

I pulled the step stool over and assigned Mia the task of spooning little blobs of the vegetable mixture onto the dough. I reached for the first strip and the whole plateful came with it. How could this happen?! I had used about two cupfuls of extra flour when rolling them out, they were positively powdery!! Sighing deeply, I halted my little helper in her tracks and rolled and cut the dough again.

Finally we were ready to start.

"Put it right there, please," I instructed, pointing to the left side of the strip. Mia spooned a pea and two potato cubes onto it. "A little more," I encouraged. Another pea. "More than that, sweetheart."

She plopped a heartier splotch onto the target. I consorted with the recipe which was becoming slightly opaque from the spattering oil heating in the pan on the stovetop. Wrap the dough four times until the filling is sealed. No problem! I flipped the dough and the curried stuffing oozed out on all sides. I scooped it back into the precarious pocket and continued folding. It looked like a beanbag with mumps.

"What are these called, Mommy?" Mia inquired.

"Samoosas, love," I said. "We're bringing them to Uncle Stuart and Ann's house for a picnic."

"You're doing a great job, Mom!" Mia praised, "I'm sure Uncle Stuart and Ann will love these mooses!"

We produced several more vegetarian hackey sacks. The kitchen was officially a disaster area: flour billowing from the counter had coated most of the surfaces as if a cocaine-addicted goliath had sneezed a few kilos into the air before he'd had a chance to snort it. The sink was piled up with mixing bowls, measuring cups and various utensils that hadn't seen the light of day since I'd bought them.

After finally squeezing out a perfect strip, I jerked the rolling pin away too quickly and the remaining dough dislodged itself, flew into the air and unceremoniously flapped onto the floor. It was now 2:50 p.m., and I still had to fry the samoosas, change Mia, change myself, and leave the house by 3:30 p.m.

I released Mia from duty, took the dough balls over to the stove and found that they had adhered to each other again. Too tired to start over and up against the wall for time, I began tugging them apart and squishing them back together where necessary to keep them sealed.

Now closely resembling the fake testicles with tumors we passed around in my college health class, the samoosas were eased into the oil and they sizzled wildly, jerking around erratically. I underestimated how quickly oil heats to the temperature of an erupting volcano and within seconds they had surpassed golden brown and were heading into char-town. Flipping them about uselessly, I wrangled the scorched pastries onto a plate lined with paper towels to drain.

One particular specimen began to unwrap itself and its resulting tail promptly puffed out like a bullfrog competing for a mate. I managed to separate the inflated pillow from the rest of the hors d' oeuvre and fished it out of the boiling liquid.

3:05 p.m. I surveyed the damage. My hair was a greasy wreck and my clothes were coated in a fine dusting of powdery flour. My fingers were yellow from the curry powder and I was, in a word, unfit, for an afternoon gathering amongst other human beings.

The shower was a complete blur and progress came to a standstill briefly when I realized it had come down to a judgment between the two clean items in my closet: a t-shirt paired with jeans that were too small, or a sleeveless crepe dress that I'd never bothered to shorten and thus was at least 6 inches too long and so had a train. Most women would have called in their regrets at this stage rather than be seen in either of these statements. On second thought, most women would not have let the situation reach the stage where these were their only options.

However, my procrastination didn't allow for a self-beration session and I decided there were enough bulging bags accompanying my daughter and I to our dinner venue without inflicting muffin tops upon the crowd as well. I said a quick prayer that I wouldn't break my neck tripping over my own trailing hemline and gathered up my copilot and sautéed moose balls.

Most of the guests gallantly made their way through them but it was pretty obvious they were not the hit of the hour.

I have a new, profound respect for Malaysian women who subject themselves to this undertaking on a daily basis and moreover, make their product look as good as it tastes.

It is also apparent that perhaps I would be more successful in future attending potlucks with slightly less complicated themes. I imagine I might just be able to pull off "Gummy Worms," "Fruit" or, if all else fails, "Water."

BYE-BYE BINKY

Along with all the other terrible things that we were never going to let our child have, a binky seemed like the infant version of cigarettes; a nasty habit, something to keep the orthodontists in business and create unnecessary dependence in our child.

But by the time I woke up from my C-section, my tiny bundle was already plugged with a yellow Nuk, and a love affair was born.

For a while, our house was littered with pacifiers. We couldn't take two steps without standing on one, they were scattered in our daughter's crib like a spilled bag of popcorn, always just a small stretch away. Her car seat and stroller were fully equipped with these little rubber and plastic plugs. They were the highest priority items and we never, ever left the house without them. My daughter would have been content to sit in a soiled diaper for a week, but hell hath no fury like our binkyless baby.

Binkies came and went and between the upgrades to

new sizes and losing them, leaving them places and accidentally sacrificing some to places like public restroom floors, we spent the equivalent of a part-time salary on them. Mia became a paci connoisseur and favored certain brands over others.

However, in a pinch, she would settle and was willing to take what she could get.

There was always a reason why binky couldn't go: a cold, a change in schedule, an airplane trip, a boo boo. I hated that stinky germ magnet, but Mia was so in love with it and it calmed her so completely that we couldn't bear to subject her to the inevitable. At 9 months, her first word was "bikky."

I rationalized that at least she wasn't sucking her thumb: you can't exactly take your child's thumb away when the time to part came nigh.

Like an addict trying to start a twelve step program, there were several attempts to wean Mia from the love of her life. We were finally down to one, known simply as the blue binky, and it was relegated to her bed only.

There was a toy guitar that she had coveted for several months. Finally, sensing an opportunity for some leverage, I tried to strike a bargain.

"There are babies who don't have any binkies and they cry themselves to sleep at night. Don't you want to give yours to them?" I suggested. "If you give your binky to the babies, you can have a guitar," I sing songed, hoping this carrot would be just attractive enough to do the trick. But Mia recoiled in horror.

"This is *my* binky," she said, her eyebrows knitted in

concern. I knew not to press that point, and several more months passed by. Every night I would go to kiss my child goodnight and get a plastic knob in my face. She could work that binky like a parasol twirler in an old broadway musical.

One morning, I went in to get her and she was ready for me. With a bright smile, her hands cupped together, she extended her arms and presented me with her most prized possession. "I want to give this to the babies," she announced. I was thrilled.

"I'm so proud of you, sweetheart!!! Let's go and get a guitar!!" I exclaimed.

"Okay, Mommy!" she beamed. Before she could change her mind, I raced her to Toys R Us and purchased her reward. She played with it all the way home, and it sat next to her when she had lunch. All was good until nap time loomed large.

Mia climbed into her bed and began scrubbling around in the covers. "Where's my binky?" she inquired.

"Mia, you gave it to the babies so you could have your guitar, remember?" I prodded, hoping this would settle it.

I could see the panic clouding her face. "But I want it!" she said, her voice a little more shrill.

"But sweetheart, now you have a guitar!" I said.

Mia burst out crying. "I don't want a guitar!!" she wailed. "I want my binky back!" She buried her face in her pillow, sobbing hysterically.

I rubbed her back while she wept, thinking it would

subside after a few minutes. But her pitch and fervor intensified until she was gasping for breath.

"I...w...want...m...m...my...bi....binky..." she spluttered, choking on the very air she was struggling to inhale.

Clearly, I was at a crossroad. Did I stand my ground and force the issue? Or give the binky back but with the condition that the guitar went away?

In violation of probably every child-rearing book in print today, I decided to go with the latter.

"Okay, love, you can have your binky back but then no guitar. Do you want your binky or a guitar?"

The weight of this choice sat on her head for a moment or two and her little face contorted in pain as she tried to stifle another sob. My heart positively ached for her. I wondered how many hours on the psychologist's couch I had just added to her future plate.

"Binky," she whispered, and I obliged, retrieving the disgusting pacifier, kicking myself for not actually throwing it away earlier that day, and then for not sticking to my guns.

They were reunited like star-crossed lovers and she drifted off to a deep, sated sleep.

Many more months went by. Periodically Mia would ask for her guitar but I held firm. No guitar until she gave her binky to the babies. I began to despair and again I berated myself for blowing a perfect opportunity to get rid of it.

But time has a funny way of working things out, and

eventually fate intervened. One night well after her third birthday, we had completed almost all of the bedtime routine, and Mia clamored into her bed. As always, she began searching for the Blue Binky, but it was nowhere to be found.

"Where's my binky, Mommy?" she asked.

"I don't know, let's see," I responded. I had a gut feeling, a glimmer of instinctive guidance, that this could be it. This could be the night we got rid of the BB for good. I dutifully helped her look and knew that it was most likely under the bed, or hiding in the equivalent of the San Diego zoo of stuffed animals on her bed.

But I latched onto this second chance like a pitbull on an intruder. "I think the binky is gone," I observed.

Incredulously, this time there were no tears. "Gone?" she repeated.

"Gone, love. I think it's time to say goodbye to the binky, we can't find it, and you're a big girl now."

I forgot that small people exist in an accelerated learning pattern, like dog years. Apparently the recent months had matured my daughter enough to understand this concept and what's more, accept it.

"But you can have your guitar now!" I trilled, smiling broadly.

"GUITAR?!?" Her smile was ear to ear and her eyes were dancing. "Thanks Mom!!!"

Despite the fact that we were on step 40 of 42 of the bedtime routine and it was already a little past eight o'clock, I ran to get the guitar and let her serenade me for several minutes before telling her it was time to go to bed.

I held my breath when it came to the goodnight kiss but all went without incident.

The next night there was a little anxiety when she remembered there was no more binky. This time I let her snivel it out but it didn't last long, and was even more fleeting the next night. By night three, binky was a bygone, a guest star in most of her baby pictures that, like her bibs and swaddling blankets, was now a closed chapter of her infancy.

Despite my disdain for the binky, it had been such an integral part of Mia's first years that I thought I would actually have a sentimental reaction to seeing its disappearance. However, what I felt instead on Mia's behalf was a sense of accomplishment, and an awed appreciation for much she'd grown emotionally.

Now, if we could just get her to sit on the potty…

BLOOD DONOR

I am the universal receiver. My rare blood type means that, in a life-threatening emergency, I can take blood from pretty much anyone.

Therefore, I feel it's my civic and karmic duty to give back, and attempt to donate whenever possible. The slightly sticky thing is, I have veins the thickness of sewing thread. They are as uncooperative as a teenager who needs to do his homework.

Once, after a particularly drawn-out blood giving episode at work, I did manage to make it back to the general vicinity of my department before I passed out in the middle of the floor. Adding to my mortification was the fact that I continued to black out every time I sat up. I eventually managed to army crawl my way back to my desk and lay on the floor for a couple more hours until my workmates had fed me enough sugar so that I could get back into my chair.

Several years later, I was ready to try it again, and signed up for a time slot with the American Red Cross.

The bloodmobile was stationed across the parking lot and I jaunted over to fill out my paperwork. It turned out that there was a bit of a line ahead of me, so I settled in with the booklet and started scribbling.

Had I ever tested positive for HIV? Did I have any sexually transmitted diseases? Had I ever held hands with, looked in the general direction of, or thought about possibly becoming intimate with a man who had a) lived in a third world country b) eaten meat in Great Britain c) participated in random pornographic activities with prostitutes d) basically ever set foot outside a monastery? Was I anemic? Did I have hepatitis? Ever stubbed my toe? Ever sat next to someone who could locate Africa on a map?

I turned in the questionnaire and asked the volunteer how long the estimated wait time was. He guessed about thirty minutes, and assured me I was welcome to walk around a bit if I liked. As I was completing this transaction a woman in a lab coat bounded out of the bathroom and over to the table and asked where the bloodmobile was. The gentleman pointed her in the direction of the RV and she bolted outside.

He and I exchanged looks and I felt my left eyebrow rise until it was about two millimeters under my hairline.

"Well that doesn't inspire much confidence!" I confessed. If she can't find the bus where she's been working all morning, how is she supposed to find a vein?!"

The man chuckled and said, "I bet you'll get her,

too!" When they finally called me up, he smiled and said, "Good luck."

I was led around the side of the building and was greeted by the smell of exhaust fumes and the rumble of the generator. I was ushered up the steps and into one of the suffocatingly small rooms where a poor man was sweating profusely. He closed the door and we began the question and answer ritual to get all the information into the computer. A kind soul, the man was very sweet but his hunt and peck typing style was adding copious minutes to the time away from my desk, as well as building my apprehension that the directionally challenged phlebotomist would be calling my name any second.

Eventually we got to the part where he pierced my finger and coerced a drop of blood out of it to see if I had enough iron to proceed. He deposited it into the vial of solution where it promptly sank like a stone. I was cleared for takeoff, and if I would please wait there, someone would be right with me to pretend I was a human pincushion and drain the life force from my veins.

Lo and behold, a minute later for a reason I can only now understand was to write this story, who should pop her friendly face in the door but the very person I had been dreading yet very much anticipating.

Like a lamb to the slaughter I followed her out to one of the gurneys and climbed onto the naugahide. She prodded my arms for a bit as if she were picking out avocados in the produce section at the grocery store.

Satisfied with her selection, she swabbed my arm with iodine and got the equipment.

I usually watch the whole thing but this time I turned my head away to look out the window, trying to calm my thoughts and find my happy place. By the time I turned my head back towards her, I had only time to see the needle, which was approximately the size of a lead pipe, and not enough to verbalize the "NOOOOOOOOOOOOOO" that was on the tip of my tongue.

I watched in slow motion as the cylinder ripped through my skin and sank into my flesh. Blood splattered into the bag and promptly stopped.

"Come on," she coaxed as she stirred the needle around a little, trying to get the flow going. I suppressed the tsunami of nausea and knew it was all over.

"Um," I trembled queasily, "I think the vein has collapsed."

"That happens sometimes," replied the Jack the Ripper of blood procurement. "The needle sometimes gets a plug of skin and it blocks the hole."

Yes, I snarked to myself, I suppose that tends to happen when you use a hypodermic HOSE instead of a normal-sized needle.

She cleared away the bag that would never reach its potential and told me to have a cookie and some juice anyway. Next to the bag of butter cookies was The Sticker, the consolation prize of the donation deadbeats. "Be nice to me today, I tried to give blood."

What I want to know is, where was the sticker that said "Be nice to me today, I tried to find a vein?"

OUT OF THE MOUTHS OF BABES

Every parent goes through this in one form or another, at one time or another. Yet just because something is a rite of passage doesn't make it less excruciating when it's your own child, your proverbial turn at bat.

The silver lining, if one was to look for it, was the fact that we were in the grocery store. At one time I believed grocery stores hired children to randomly cry and throw temper tantrums in the aisles, as at any given time there is always at least one child in the midst of a grand mal meltdown. Being an employee in that environment must surely mean that one is a little inured to the sound of small, shrieking voices and the little people from whence they come in general, and perhaps a little more understanding as to what comes forth from their gloriously unpredictable mouths.

My daughter, although not sobbing or flinging herself onto the ground like some of her peers in an over-tired last ditch effort to get her parent to say yes to something at the cash register, was hopping about in bored, typical fashion.

I began to load our items onto the conveyor belt.

"Mom," said Mia, clamoring up and down the wheel base of the cart like she was in a step aerobics class, "Can we have this flashlight?"

"No, sweetheart," I answered, "We have enough flashlights at home."

"Please, Mom? We don't have one like THIS! All my friends would LOVE this one. Pleeeeease?"

"I know, Mia, but the ones we do have are just fine. The answer is no."

I continued unpacking my cart. Mia was considerably quiet all of a sudden, so, enjoying the chit chat holiday for a moment, I worked more efficiently in the blissful respite. Popping the last of the tissue boxes on the belt, I glanced over at my daughter.

Her eyes were wide and transfixed; her mouth slightly agape. She blinked slowly, and I could see the wheels were turning furiously in her head. I followed her gaze and what I saw sent shivers down my spine in dreaded anticipation.

The poor female cashier had a balding head. Hers was not the slightly thinning variety either; the receding tide had ebbed and there had apparently not been a reciprocal flow for quite some time.

I literally held my breath.

"Mom," Mia began, her eyes still glued to our cashier.

"Not now, honey," I shot back nonchalantly, my heart pounding a little. "I just have to concentrate right now."

The woman and I made eye contact and smiled at each other. "Hi, how are you?" she asked sweetly.

"Fine thanks, how about you?" I replied.

"I'm good," she said.

"Mooohhhhm?" it came again, a little more insistent.

"Mia, not now!" I desperately tried again. I moved to the credit card machine as the woman slowly rang up my purchases, hoping to distract my youngster, as she loves to swipe my card for me and thought maybe she'd want to do so now. "Why don't you help me with the credit card?"

But the train had left the station.

"Is that a lady or a man?" she inquired.

I winced, and did the only thing that came to mind. I completely ignored her, and hoped to God that there was enough background noise to cover up her remark. Not my contribution to nomination for mother of the year, I know, but I was too deep in mortification mode to react any other way.

This was the second incident of its kind at this very store. The previous run-in had involved a liberally tattooed cashier whose earlobes were stretched quite significantly from the huge plastic discs lodged within them, and who also had a large bolt protruding from each side of his bottom lip. Mia's assessment of this gentleman was, "Mommy! He looks like a monster!" After I hissed at her and gave her the SHUSH face, she responded with a contrite smile and sweetly said, "Well he looks like a *nice* monster."

There are naturally several options for dealing with this kind of occasion in future. I could try and check out the checker more carefully to head this off at the pass by simply choosing another checkout line, or keep at least a pound of salt water taffy in my purse at all times so that I can shove several pieces of them into her mouth at once when I hear the first "Mom." Or, I could use this opportunity to teach her that even if someone has a horn growing out of their left cheek, an arm where one of their ears should be, or three eyeballs, she needs to hold her tongue.

As soon as we exited the building, I pulled the cart over to the side to give my daughter a little lesson in the art of being tactful. I knelt down so that our faces were level.

"Mia," I said, "It's not nice to say things like 'is that a lady or a man' because it can hurt the lady's feelings." In fairness to Mia since she is very young, and the woman did have a very sparsely sowed scalp, I could understand a small child's confusion so I gave her an out. "In future, even if you notice something like that and you want to tell me or ask me about it, please wait until we get outside. Okay?"

"Okay Mom," she agreed. "I promise."

This particular cringe-fest had officially come to a close, and to her credit, my daughter has made good on her promise so far. In a recent outing to a frozen yogurt store Mia asked if she could tell me a secret. I immediately took her up on her offer, expecting the sweet, hotly breathed "I love you" into my ear as usual.

Cupping her hand around my lobe, and punctuated with giggles and chortles as she spoke, she uttered, "That man has holes in his shirt for his boobies to stick through," and then giving in and cackling in a stage whisper, "What a weirdo!"

On another occasion she did have the grace to wait for the sanctity of our living room before asking me what a douche-bag was.

However, as a parent of a little one, it's never truly over.

One merely lives from one event to the next, hoping that your child will not publicly repeat in perfect context all the filthy swear words they hear at home, or ask completely inappropriate questions about private body parts in front of your boss, or remark about others' misfortunes or shortcomings in front of them.

Therefore one can only take a deep breath and wait for it in terrible suspense, and be sure to write it all down for future entertainment when it does inevitably unfold.

I'm personally still considering the taffy alternative.

JUST LET GO

I'd been fighting this cold for weeks and finally lost the battle. My herbal rescue wonder formula that usually kicks the crap out of colds to the point that I barely feel it just wasn't a match for this one.

I was going through the bedtime routine with Mia and could feel the tickle in the back of my throat getting worse with each breath. I didn't want to spray the poor child with my infestation although I realized she was probably harboring it by now as well. But the strangulated words that squeaked through my hoarse vocal chords were getting increasingly more difficult to push out and I had to admit defeat. I leapt out of her bed and ran to grab a cough drop.

I returned to her room I could see the concern on Mia's face and remembered how I felt as a small child on the rare occasions that my parents were sick.

"O..kay, goo(AHEAAAAHM)dnight, Mi (rattle)a! I can't (dissolving into a whisper) talk anymore," I spluttered.

"But you didn't rock me," she said, her bottom lip slightly curled under, her forlorn face downward, shoulders hunched forward a little.

"Just for a (wheeze, hack) minute, sweetheart. Then it's (bark, bark) bedtime," I said.

Mia   climbed over the bedrail and into my arms. We rocked very gently while I tried to control my breathing without erupting.

"What are you eating, Mommy?" she asked.

It was starting to work. "A cough drop," I answered.

"Is that candy?" she perked up.

"No, it's like medicine to help my throat feel better," I explained.

"Does it taste yummy?" she inquired. This is the child who thanks me after I give her cough medicine and asks for more.

"Not really," I said. "It's not horrible, but it's not great. It's not really supposed to taste good."

"Mommy, I'll rub your throat to make you feel better!" Mia offered. She began lightly patting my chest as we rocked.

"Thank you, sweetheart," I smiled at her. She pursed up her lips and cocked her head to the side a little, an idea brewing.

"Would you like a band aid, Mommy?" She asked. "That would make you feel better!"

"I would love one, thank you!" I replied. She interrupted the patting for a moment to peel the imaginary band aid and plaster it on my clavicle.

"Mommy, did you swallow your medicine?" she asked.

"No, love, this isn't the kind of medicine you swallow. This has to slowly melt on your tongue."

She wasn't buying it. "Mommy, you have to swallow the medicine! That's why your throat is still coughing! Just let it go, Mom, you have to let it go. Then you won't be sick anymore." She resumed her patting.

I stopped rocking and stared at my daughter, her sleepy, lushly lashed hazel eyes looking back at me. "Just let it go, Mom, then your cough will go away," she repeated.

I was struck. This three and a half year old girl couldn't have possibly known that she totally hit the nail on the head. I did need to let it go. All of it. The stress and worry and must-dos and mustn't says, and fretting about silly things really *was* making me sick.

While I knew she was really talking about my cough drop, my daughter's profound statement got through to me and was the slap upside of the head that I needed.

"You're absolutely right, Mia," I told her. "I do need to let it go. Thank you, you are a very, very sweet little girl. And you know something? You really did make me feel better. See? I'm not coughing anymore."

She blinked and smiled. "Yes, you're not coughing anymore!" she acknowledged. "I'm going to be a doctor like Uncle Jeremy when I grow up," she announced.

"I think you would be a wonderful doctor, my

love," I agreed. I plopped her into bed and gave her a huge hug.

What would I do without this child? People often tell me how hard it is to be a parent, and how much work it takes on a daily basis to keep things together. While of course I admit there are exasperating moments here and there, for me, Mia is all the medicine I need.

There is a school of thought that your children choose you for the lessons you will teach them in this life, but I have discovered the opposite to be true. I have learned more about patience from this little person than I could possibly offer her in return, and each day my capacity to love is expanded even further to a depth I didn't know existed.

Now, if I could just wrap *that* up in lozenge form and sell it!

OFF THE CHARTS

To be completely honest, I really hate gyms. I also hate most forms of exercise; it's just such a lot of exertion. There is another reason why I can't stand those human hamster wheel hangars, and it is probably the most compelling reason I have avoided them like the plague they are.

I am not one of those lithe giraffe-women, who wear the perfectly coordinated yoga pants and tank top, with a flawless face full of makeup, who manage to get their hair bound up into one of those sexy, perfectly tousled ponytails that bounce like a horse's mane as they run on the treadmill or climb the stairmaster for two hours and never drop a bead of sweat.

No, I am the girl on the last treadmill in the row, drenched in sweat that is pouring into my eyes, matting my damp hair to my ruddy, puffing cheeks in whatever sweats and non-clingy T-shirt I could find that still fit. While Workout Barbie keeps her complexion peaches and cream (or whatever shade of foundation she slathered on with a spackle trowel prior to heading out the door) and smelling just as pleasant, I reek like the stench of a thousand baboon armpits after the first few minutes.

During my very first ever yoga class, my concentration was interrupted by what I thought to be a broken water main above my mat. Upon further inspection I discovered the torrent of water *dripping* onto the mat was actually being evicted by my sweat glands, something I didn't know was possible in such substantial quantities from human skin.

At one point, the instructor, a breathtakingly gorgeous man, made the rounds to give everyone a little massage and I cringed at the thought of him laying his magnificent hands on my clammy neck and worse, keeling over from the smell of eau de eew assaulting his senses when he got near.

But, it was clearly time to do something active, so I called one of the national franchises to find out if they had kickboxing classes. I got through to a very eager gentleman named Chris. All I really wanted to know was did they have the classes. But Chris was insistent that I come to the gym and he would show me around. I reluctantly agreed and we set up the appointment.

I arrived at my scheduled time and had to wait at the front desk for my knight in shining spandex. Glancing around at the trainers, I pegged him immediately for the tall, sculpted He-man schmoozing a huge, buff guy at the free weights. I braced myself and waited patiently for him to pat the guy on the back and come striding over to me.

His smile was ear to ear in that slimy, I'm-about-to-catch-myself-a-sucker kind of way. I wondered if he practiced cranking it up in front of the mirror before he left for work.

"Romi?" he boomed, extending his arm and squeezing my hand in that I'm-supposed-to-squeeze-assertively handshake.

"Hi," I smiled self-consciously, pumping his hand back in return, suppressing the urge to pretend I had socks to fold and bolting for the door.

"Let's get a little history, what exactly are you looking for?" he eyed me up and down. A mere reflex, particularly in his line of work, but it irritated me nevertheless.

I explained that I was not really that into going to the gym, but I was interested in kickboxing classes, thinking it would be a fun way to relieve stress and also attempt to rescue my waistline from its woeful state.

He nodded and ushered me over to the scale. By this time, another young specimen from the isle of pumpletude materialized and the interrogation began. They recorded my weight, measured my height and brought out an apparatus that looked like a sinister pair of barbeque tongs. Before I had a chance to blink, the tongs were clamping my stomach and the skin on my back between my shoulder blades like a drug-sniffing canine that had just discovered a gigantic bag of weed.

Chris and Adonis Boy brought out a chart and, eyebrows full of practiced concern, held it up on the wall in front of me.

"I hope you have good insurance!" Chris lamented. "You have 47% body fat!"

"Here's the chart," double-teamed his colleague, pointing to the red, you're-a-walking-heart-attack section of the chart, "And here's you!" He motioned to an empty space on the wall under the bottom of the paper, pausing slightly for effect. "You're off the charts."

My blood pressure is ninety over sixty-five and at this particular point in time, I weighed one hundred and twenty eight pounds. I was still processing this ridiculous assessment of my health when a third vulture swooped into the party with an appointment book.

"We need to get you in for personal training sessions right away!" he gushed, frantically flipping through the book to the next available slot, struggling valiantly to save my life, which according to these gentlemen, was in mortal, desperate danger. "How soon can you come in?" He stared wide-eyed at me, his pen poised over the page.

I stared back at the man, half expecting him to ask what he had to do to get me in the car today and then remembered I wasn't actually in a used car lot.

"I'm going to have to think about this," I tried to stop the train.

"What's to think about?" barreled Chris, "Don't you care about your health? What's more important than that?"

I fervently wished I had mace, I would have sprayed

all three of them. I smiled as sweetly as I could and explained that I was leaving.

In a last-ditch effort, Chris pressed his business card into my hand, and urged me to call him as soon as possible. I went home feeling like I needed a shower to rinse the filth of frenzied sales pressure off my skin.

However, this didn't solve my problem. I still wanted to take kickboxing classes and this was the only gym I could find that offered a month to month contract. After a little more research, I found another location closer to my house and decided I was going to enroll after all.

I marched through the doors and right up to the smiling young boy behind the counter. "I want to sign up," I said.

"Would you like a tour of the gym?" he offered politely.

"No. I would not," I snapped frostily and glared at him with what must have come across as an icy laser beam. I watched the smile melt off his face and think I heard the sound of a needle skipping off the record.

"O…kay," he said, "let's go sit down."

He ushered me to a desk and logged into the computer. There was no idle chit chat and his fingers flew furiously across the keyboard as I curtly answered his questions. I knew I was being a complete bitch and finally had to give the poor kid a break.

"Thank you for not pushing me," I said and offered an apologetic smile.

"That's okay," he grinned back, "I could tell you just

weren't having any of it." I was about to launch into the whole saga, and clarify that I wasn't in the mood to have another run-in with the gymnasium jaws of life, but I didn't even have the energy to bore him with the details.

We finished our transaction and I was officially signed up. I went away from the table with my temporary pass in hand.

Here's to you, Chris, I thought as I left, waving my pass skyward. Who's the sucker now?!

WORMIE

We had already picked out the carpet, and the measurements had been taken. All that remained was to go into the hardware store and give them our credit card to seal the deal.

Mia and I arrived at the flooring counter to find it deserted; the store associates were on their lunch breaks. A gentleman from another department came over to help us but it quickly became apparent that I was really going to have to wait for the flooring guy. To make good use of the wait, I decided to do a return and poke around with Mia for a bit.

The associate at the return counter and I chit chatted a little and she casually mentioned the summer accessories they had got in. One of these was a little ceramic worm to put in the soil next to your plants that changes color slightly to tell you when the plants have had enough water and alternately changes back when they need more.

Given that my poor plants survive in a constant

precarious state of moderate to severe dehydration, I thought this was a fabulous idea and Mia was taken with the idea of putting worms in our garden.

We located the box of "Wormies" and Mia was a bit disappointed to see they weren't real. Nevertheless, we took two for starters; I figured if they really did help I would come back in the summer and stock up.

They were essentially just tubes of terra cotta with little faces painted on them, and the basic principle was simple. When they got wet they would turn a deeper rusty orange, and conversely when they dried out, would return to their lighter, chalky hue.

Mia insisted on holding them and I told her to be careful as they would break if dropped on the floor. She pledged to be vigilant, and I handed them to her, wondering how long it would take before one or both took a tumble.

We made it back to the flooring counter, and to her credit, it took longer than I anticipated before one inevitably slipped out of the tag and instantly became 3 larger pieces with a few crumbly fragments as it met the floor.

I sighed, and scooped the humpty dumpty of the worm world off the linoleum. I looked over at Mia who had her hands over her ears, and her eyes were round with concern.

"I'm sorry, Mommy!" she said, instantly repentant.

"That's okay, Mia," I replied, a little miffed at myself for allowing her to hold them when I had clearly seen this coming.

"Accidents happen!" she sing-songed, referring to the mantra she picked up while watching potty training videos and which we had used over and over to try and reassure her that accidents do, indeed, happen to everyone at some time or another. "Mom, we can fix it, right?" she asked, her eyebrows still bunched a little. "Let's just show the other one to Daddy so he doesn't see."

"Honey, it doesn't matter," I told her. "Yes, accidents do happen, but we still need to try and be careful with things. And Mia, we don't need to hide this from Daddy, he knows accidents happen too. If we break things, we don't have to hide it and pretend it didn't happen, we need to tell our mommies and daddies, even if they get mad at us sometimes."

To take full advantage of this opportunity, I added, "And sometimes we can fix things, and sometimes we can't, it depends on what it is." I didn't want to put the fear of God in this poor child over a $1.50 piece of pottery, but at the same time I want her to grow up with a respect for things.

I could see in her face she was still fretting. "I'm not mad, Mia, it's alright."

"We can fix this, Mommy!" she decided. "I have glue at home and I'll fix it right away when we get home!" She thought for a minute and added, "When things break, we just fix them, right Mama?"

I stifled a chuckle and told her again that it was o kay. "Mom, if you break something, it's okay, you can tell me and I won't be mad at you!" she reassured me. I gave her a hug and kissed the top of her head.

"Thank you, love," I responded.

We got through the paperwork and the manager took us to the cash register to ring up the sale. I carefully placed the worm and clay chunks on the counter and took out my credit card.

"Worms!" exclaimed the cashier, smiling at Mia, "My niece LOVES worms!" We smiled back and then the woman noticed the unfortunate fate that had befallen Wormie just a few minutes before. "Oh! This one's broken!" she remarked. "Would you like one a new one?" she kindly offered.

I smiled and shook my head, "No. Thanks though." I wanted to take the broken one home. Firstly, my upbringing made me feel obligated to pay for the one we had broken, but more importantly, I wanted Mia to understand that we have to live with the consequences of our actions even if they aren't intentional.

On the ride home, Mia again detailed how she would fix the worm when we got home. To be honest, the more I thought about it, it actually helped that we technically now had four little bits of wormie rather than two; we could now spread the wealth around a little more. I said as much to my child, who held the remaining whole worm very gingerly in both hands all the way home.

When we got home, my husband was getting ready for work. "Daddy, daddy! The worm broke but I'm going to fix him with glue!" she barged into the bathroom where he was finishing up in the shower.

"Oh wow, that's great," he replied benignly over the roar of the shower head.

"Then we can put him in the garden to help our plants!" she went on.

"Sounds good," he said comfortingly.

Buoyed by his encouraging response, she went downstairs and headed for her little art table in the kitchen.

"Mom, can you help me glue him back together?" she implored.

I was focused on getting lunch together for her, so didn't look round as I chopped up cucumber onto her melamine plate.

"Actually, if we leave him broken then we can use it for four plants instead of two," I said. "That way we'll cover more plants!"

"Mom, please, pleeeeeaaase help me stick him back together!" she pleaded. I turned around to face her.

She had already twisted open the lid of the Elmer's school glue and was poised with the glue in one hand and the middle segment of Wormie's broken body in the other. I opened my mouth to tell her that Elmer's was probably not going to hold the terra cotta together, and even if it did temporarily do the trick, most likely wouldn't stand the test of a few waterings once we put it in the soil. And then just as quickly, I shut it.

It dawned on me that this was not simply a case of my daughter ignoring my advice, and the fact that it wasn't the "right" glue didn't matter. She needed to fix what she had broken, to take responsibility for her accident, and I needed to help her do this.

I held the affected part while she squeezed a blob of adhesive onto it. "Okay, put his head back on," she instructed.

Despite a small chip that was unsalvageable, the head fit back on effortlessly and slid into place as the jagged edges met each other like cog teeth interlocking. I wiped the excess glue off with my finger and held the other side while she dropped another sticky blob on that end. I reached for the tail but was intercepted.

"I want to do it, Mom." she stated.

I let her put the tail on and then rotated it to fit when she turned her head away for a second.

"See? I KNEW we could fix it, Mom!" she said proudly. Her relief was palpable, a sense of calm now that she had restored Wormie to his original shape. This loop closed, her face relaxed and she scampered off to the living room.

As I put the worm on the table to dry, I was proud of her too; impressed with her courage to own up to the incident, determination to see it rectified and the fact that she had got the message.

However, she wasn't the only one who learned a lesson. I was struck by how suddenly the teaching moments pop up, and that sometimes they are so subtle you can easily miss them if you aren't paying attention. I also learned how heavily one's own reaction factors into the equation and sets the stage for our children's future coping mechanisms. But more importantly, I saw how critical it is that I let my daughter make her own mistakes and correct them for herself.

There will be many more Wormies to come. When they do, we will be ready with the Elmer's.

CONTINUING EDUCATION

Unfortunately I'd done it again.

The quiet pit gnawing at my gut told me this was shaping up to be a reprisal of the time I took the calculus class in college to satisfy my math requirement because for some obscure reason I tested into it, and thought I would be worthy of the challenge.

The other students also pursuing an acting degree with me took the math 151 class and didn't have the pleasure of standing in the registrar's office, whooping out loud at the D- on their report card once the class was over, shaking with relief because they, by the skin of their teeth and some impressive bell curve grading, had actually passed. This blight on my record denoted the one quarter of twelve where I didn't make the Dean's list.

That torturous class was captained by an incredibly brilliant mathematician, whose mastery of his subject matter was directly and inversely proportionate to his inability to explain it. The poor man couldn't have made calculus stick in my head if he'd written it on a dart and lodged it in my left temple.

Indeed, whenever I asked him a question I found myself falling deeper into the depths of complete mathematical despair, as his mottled response invariably only served to push me further into a void of total incomprehension. I owe said D- then, to one of my fellow school of theatre buddies, who sat up with me the entire night before the final, and got me to see enough of a sliver of the light in order to squeak by and cross this dreadful requirement off my list.

There are things each of us does well. These are the things that come to us almost as easily as breathing, the things we make appear effortless to others. I can sing on key, construct a reasonably coherent sentence and have been known to cut a rug or two. I am compassionate, a patient mother, and possess strong problem solving and analytical skills.

I am also hopelessly right-brained, and I make my living as a business analyst. Furthermore, it appears that after thirty six years, I still simply can't pass up a good challenge.

Thus, having learned SQL reporting language on the fly from my very patient and humble work mates (who spent their own college years learning IT programming as opposed to perfecting tongue twisters such as the one about Betty Botter who bought some butter), I felt a more solid base was in order; a platform on which to build my budding skill set. After acquiring the necessary approvals from my boss and his boss, I enrolled in a five week online SQL class through an accredited establishment of hallowed secondary education.

My student advisor patiently waited while I reset my forgotten user ID and then password respectively, and then walked me through the online environment. I must admit I felt the familiar pangs of oh-what-have-I-done creeping in but I duly tossed them aside and told myself I would be fine.

The first day of class, I meandered through the chats and posts, feeling increasingly like a lost fart in a perfume factory. An implicit game of one-upmanship was going on, as everyone tried to out-IT each other with impressive tech-speak that whizzed over my head with the same speed as the new processors they were throwing about in their diatribes. A clatch of people who had apparently worked with each other in these classes several times before immediately asked to be placed together in a team for this class.

Teams. UGH. I am all for teamwork when I'm at work, but what I was really looking for here was a quiet way to soak up information without having to be the last kid picked for the blue team in PE class.

While we were told students not requesting a specific team would be grouped by time zone, I did notice the majority of my fellow enrollees are on the east coast, and began to be a bit concerned as to when I was going to fit in this time commitment. Did I do it *before* waking up at 5:45 a.m., giving my daughter breakfast, getting her dressed, taking her to school, going to work, leaving at 5:30 p.m. to pick her up, giving

161

her dinner, bathing her and getting her to bed? Or did I do it *after* her bedtime? Would my east coast cohorts please be so kind as to work with me from midnight until they passed out from exhaustion to accommodate my schedule?

I had specifically signed up for what I believed to be a one-off class through the non-degree program. Yet almost all of my classmates' bios indicated they were working towards a degree in Information Technology.

In an attempt to post a response to the question about increasing trends in data management and how software companies were rising to meet the trend, I opened a reading assignment. My eyes began to glaze a little as concepts about data clouds and DBMSs swirled around my sphere of vision. Upon reaching the end of the first page, I realized with a sinking feeling that I was in fact reading a Martian manuscript.

After rereading the article another twelve times, and with the Mountain Standard Time witching hour closely approaching, I had to post something to satisfy the assignment deadline. I organized my thoughts as best I could and added my statement to the string already available.

To my crushing embarrassment the following day, my post had a big red U next to it – the "unsubstantive" scarlet letter of class that let me know my entry was effectively crap.

I was mortified. And stupefied. Where did I go wrong? I consulted the syllabus and was enlightened. Unsubstantive marks would be awarded for any responses under 200 words and/or not pertaining to the subject matter.

I immediately fired off an email to the instructor, asking if the issue was the former or the latter. If it was merely a matter of word count, that was easily remediable. However, if the problem stemmed from the fact that I was out in left field as far as comprehension was concerned, I had bigger fish to fry.

To my relief, his speedy response to my inquiry gave me heart: I had missed the word count. The next evening, I sat at my computer, sniveling unabashedly as I waded through the next of the Martian chronicles, unaware that my abject sorrow was abetted by the earliest of pregnancy hormones surging through my system.

We got our learning team assignments. I was paired with four other students, ranging in locales from Alaska to Phoenix. At least we were relatively close time zone-wise; however, our schedules were all over the map. Off we went, into the strange and exciting world of database creation and maintenance.

The first team assignment started a bit erratically, with each person tearing off in a direction that seemed to coincide with no-one else's. Teammates burned by other classes where their team members had shirked their responsibilities leaving them holding the bag and working overtime to get the job done were firing with all cylinders. Others were off to a slower start, unaccustomed to the more rigorous assignment deadlines of this 400-level class.

Yet despite our differing agendas at the onset, we banded together fairly quickly, and having found our rhythm, worked beautifully together over the next four weeks. Between us we created a database, built our tables, restored our .bak files and connected our dots so that we could pull meaningful data using SQL. One particular teammate was especially savvy, and her willingness to selflessly share her time and help me to get the answers on my own made her an invaluable lifeline for me as well as a new friend.

Once I got the hang of the daily participation posts, the laptop-side weeping subsided quite substantially, and I began to realize I was learning volumes, both from the instructor and also the posts of my class mates.

While I finally got the hang of translating the required hieroglyph readings, the 1:00 a.m. bedtimes were all too frequent. This coincided as per the dictates of Murphy's Law with the first trimester nausea, the combination of which wreaked untold havoc upon my green stomach.

By the time the final assignment was due, the goal of learning was temporarily suspended from my woozy vision. Like the marathon runner whose legs have given up the ghost yet continues to awkwardly lurch towards the finish line, it was all about hitting the post button to close the lid on this particular e-chapter of my educational pursuits.

Crawling into bed the following night at 8:00 p.m. was heavenly, but nothing compared to the intense feeling of satisfaction that engulfed my entire being when I received the assessment for my efforts. There it was: a magnificent A, standing proudly next to the words "final grade" like the victor in a boxing ring.

Being fifteen years older than I was the last time I had opened a text book or signed my name on a final exam paper, I could now appreciate all I had learned in this class, and how much the knowledge was in itself the point of the exercise.

But I'd also be a liar if I didn't say it just felt damn good to get that A. It appears the years haven't mellowed my competitive spirit too significantly. However if an opportunity for a redo of calculus should rear its ugly head I believe that is one challenge I will have to gracefully decline. So maybe I have come to terms with myself a little after all.

CURE FOR THE COMMON PEDICURE

The three kids were left behind with our two husbands. The cousins were so enthralled to be with each other that I don't believe they even registered we were leaving. It was the day of my brother-in-law's wedding, and my sister-in-law and I felt a little pampering was in order before we stepped into our bridesmaid dresses for the big night.

First on the agenda: a manicure and pedicure. Given that this would bring the number of pedicures I've had in my life so far to a grand total of three, I had neglected to even consider packing flip flops for our trip down to California. Hailing from Oregon, thong sandals just interfere with the webbing that grows between one's toes during the endless rainy season, so such summery notions in April were the furthest thing from my mind.

Obviously, even to a novice like me, putting tennis shoes over freshly dried nail polish is just a no-no. Thus, I flapped into the salon wearing a pair of my sister-in-law's size 10 hibiscus print flip flops, which, while perfect under her tall frame, were a little ill fitting on my size 6 feet.

Determined to not let the fact that I looked like Bozo the clown's Hawaiian cousin make me feel discomfited, I followed my sister-in-law to the friendly receptionist to let her know we were there for our appointments.

We had brought our nail polish with us. My sister-in-law explained the importance of this step: in the event a nail got accidentally scratched or chipped and needed a touch up, we would have the fix on hand at all times. I was duly impressed by this logic and expertise; again, it was something that would simply not have dawned on me.

When they called our names, I turned to see a beige leather armchair that seemed to disappear into a shallow whirlpool, swirls of warm water beckoning invitingly to my sorry feet. We nestled ourselves into the luxurious softness and my sister-in-law showed me how to turn on the various features that would probably put most people to sleep: warmth and massage to suit several preferences, catering to tired necks, backs and legs.

My pedicurist came over with her bucket of goodies. She and my sister-in-law exchanged pleasantries, and the woman was extremely nice to me, as if to say a friend of hers is a friend of mine.

It was then that I felt it was only fair to warn the poor woman that there was a teeny proviso to this treatment. Granted, asking that someone kindly not

168

touch your feet during a pedicure is rather like asking someone to drive you somewhere without turning on the ignition of the car, but I tried to impress upon her as gently as I could that I am hideously ticklish, and cannot bear the mere *suggestion* of a foot massage, let alone actually endure one.

I typically wouldn't even have consented to putting myself through this torment, but despite my general disrespect for fashion, I do have a no-ragamuffin policy for weddings, particularly when I'm in them and even more particularly when the people getting married are family.

Her eyebrows knitted together ever so slightly and she cocked her head to the side, blinking a bit. "So, no foot massage?" she asked.

"NO foot massage!!" I confirmed emphatically. "I'm REALLY ticklish so please try to just do the polish without touching my feet very much if you can."

She smiled a smile that was very friendly but I could tell she thought I was a sock short of a pair. She instructed me to put my right foot up on the bench and I dutifully, albeit reluctantly, complied. She dried my foot and then glanced at me as she wrapped her delicate fingers around the sole. I suppressed the snort that was welling up inside my throat and felt my other foot tighten into a ball in response.

With my teeth gritted and my jaw steeled, I was under the impression that I was going to hold it together. Then she moved her hand to start filing my nails. In a display of pure reflex, my leg shot out ramrod straight with the speed of a bullet and I kicked her tool bucket up into the air, missing the woman's teeth by an atom or two. It flew upwards and seemed to hang magically in midair for a second before expelling nail polish, files, cotton balls, primer, top coat and cuticle scissors like a beauty supply firework show.

The items quickly plunged into the water and the woman gasped as she fished around frantically in the froth for said soggy articles.

I cringed into my chair and began a chorus of horrified apologies. When I turned to look at my sister-in-law, I found her doubled over, clutching her stomach and laughing so hard that no sound was coming out. This of course made me start guffawing too, and the two of us rolled around, giggling and cackling like the toddlers that we'd left home with our husbands.

Finally catching her breath, my sister-in-law said, "Oh great! Now I'm going to have to find a new place to get my nails done!" This sent us into another gale of laughter while my hapless beautician tried gallantly to salvage her waterlogged tools.

I willed myself to get through the rest of the ordeal, but literally writhed and had to take several deep breaths throughout the remainder of it. Every so often an uproarious howl would emerge from my constricted throat, the kind of noise that is only wrought from a ticklish victim enduring such a procedure, or perhaps a hen being strangled half to death. Watching the woman perform a pedicure amid such a display of hysterics without so much as a single eye roll or head shake gave me a valuable lesson in the meaning of true restraint.

To be honest, the pedicure was so unbearably torturous that I don't even remember my manicure. All I know is, after I came back to my senses, I had 20 gleaming nails that were perfectly shaped, buffed and painted. I had to admit they were a far cry from the state of neglect that had befallen them prior to this extravaganza.

If it wasn't for the fact that I had almost given my pedicurist a free orthodontic treatment, I might have even considered this to be something I would voluntarily do again in the future. However, I sagely tossed that idea aside and decided to just live in the moment and struggle to enjoy it for what it was worth. I figured I had a good while until the next wedding anyway.

AND THEN THERE WERE FOUR

Just as his sister's first cries had instantly and profoundly changed our lives five years earlier, the sound of my son's newborn wail filled the operating room, and I knew that once again my whole universe had been radically altered.

Before this moment, I was a mom. Now I had children. Before, I couldn't fathom how I could possibly love another baby as fiercely as I did my daughter. Now I understood how a mother's heart fills completely for every one of her children, whether she has two or twenty-two of them.

I strained around the curtain to see my boy as they held him up, his indignant cries still ringing out in the sterile air.

When my daughter was born, I had missed the big moment, the one they drilled home week after week in my birthing class: the crucial first bonding opportunity between a mother and her child: the placing of the baby on its mother's chest immediately after birth was the gold after the long marathon of labor; the moment that, as a starry-eyed first-timer, I was led to believe would be mine to have. Because I had a c-section and my arms were out to the sides strapped down to the operating table like a gigantic T, that treasured moment eschewed me as my daughter was thrust briefly in my face and then whisked away before I really even had a chance to see her, let alone touch her.

But this time I was able to hold my second baby as they placed him on my chest. He lifted his head to look at me and our eyes met for the first time. I drank in his face: the curve of his tiny, rosebud lips, his minute but well defined nose, his deep, slate irises. He stared back in bewilderment, not sure what to make of me and all this, and probably trying to reconcile the pale, bloated woman under his nose with the voice he had heard from the inside of my belly all those months. I was struck again by the miracle of birth – here was another perfect, whole human being that I had had a hand in bringing into the world.

In stark contrast to my first delivery where I was so nauseated and drugged that I remember nothing of the recovery room, and nothing about the whereabouts of my child during that time, now I was lucid for everything: the shaking, the cold, but more importantly, my little son sleeping on my shoulder as they waited for the feeling to return to my slumbering legs.

Eventually we were moved to my room and I slept while we waited for my parents to bring Mia to the hospital to visit.

The curtain rustled and my daughter advanced

hesitantly into the room, flanked by my mom and dad. Mia was a mix of smiles and concern. She came up to the bed slowly and the IV was the first thing to catch her eye.

"Does it hurt, Mommy?" she touched my arm tenderly.

"No, sweetheart, I can't really feel it," I reassured her.

"Do you have underwear on under your hospital gown?"

I smiled. "No love."

She wanted to hold her new baby brother and enthusiastically ran to wash her hands. But when I went to hand Alex to her, she got cold feet and emphatically retracted the offer. Still, she was fascinated and sat next to her dad on the couch, smiling tenderly at her sibling. We got a photo of her kissing him on the head ever so gingerly.

The afternoon sailed by easily and I dozed off and on while my parents and husband took turns holding the baby and the nurses came in and out to take my vitals and keep up with the strict routine of ibuprofen and acetaminophen.

It was my dad who voiced the concern. "Does his mouth look a little blue to you?" he asked, looking at the sleeping newborn in his arms.

"Hmm, Mia had it too," I answered authoritatively.

"Okay," my dad said, but his brow was still furrowed.

"He seems to be breathing very fast too," he

observed.

"Yeah, Mia had the same thing," I said, recalling my daughter's rapid breathing at birth and the doctor who had talked to us about possible open heart surgery when it turned out she was absolutely fine.

We pushed the button to summon the nurse and polled her about Alex's color and breathing when she came in to check on us.

She looked at Alex and assured us that it's normal; sometimes babies take a while to adjust to life outside the womb and he was learning how to regulate his breathing. Satisfied with her assessment, we relaxed and enjoyed the afternoon with our boy.

Night fell and the nurse came in around 11:00 PM. She examined me; incision looked good, vitals were stable.

"I need to do the baby's PKU test," she said. "Should I keep him in the nursery for the night so that you can sleep?"

My intuition let off a shriek, like a sharp blow to the gut. I was about to say no, when my husband, exhausted from the cumulative effects of little sleep for months during my pregnancy when I had tossed and turned all night like a gigantic jumping bean, nodded eagerly and said, "Yes please!"

What was it? Why was I suddenly so on edge? The nurse's hospital ID badge was turned, so I couldn't see her picture or the red stripe we were told to look for to confirm that the person requesting access to our child was truly a hospital employee authorized to do so.

I felt embarrassed asking, and worse for doubting this woman, who seemed so sweet, and practically radiated kindness. But this was my child, and someone else's feelings needed to take a back seat to his safety. "I'm sorry," I smiled apologetically, "We were told to ask to see your picture and the red stripe on your ID badge."

"Of course, thank you for asking," the nurse said good-naturedly, and flipped the badge over to reveal those very items.

Yet something was gnawing at me. I just had a horrible feeling that Alex wasn't coming back that night; however, I allowed the nurse to wheel him away and tried to get some rest. We weren't to know it yet, but that nurse had just saved his life.

At two in the morning, I felt a light hand on my shoulder. My eyes flew open and the nurse who had taken Alex was at my side, her previously smiling face all business now.

"I'm sorry to have to wake you in the middle of the night to tell you this," she began, "But we're keeping your baby for tests. He is breathing very rapidly and his heart rate is double what it should be. I'm so sorry... but if it were my son, I would definitely want him checked out."

My husband was awake now too. She had our undivided attention.

"Please don't apologize!" I said. "We're so grateful that you did something about it!"

My husband helped me out of the bed and put the

non-slip socks on my steadily swelling feet. We ambled to the nursery as fast as I could go.

Clustered in the middle of the room, several bassinets were grouped next to each other like a little tot parking lot. Inside each one was a tiny swaddled infant, their soothie pacifiers rhythmically bopping up and down, the only detectible movement from this huddle of bundled burritos.

And off in the far back corner by himself, I spied my own bundle. Beneath the oxygen tent, clad in only a diaper, his doll-sized chest was wracked with retractions and he was red and sweaty from the heat lamp glowering overhead. There were wires stuck to his chest, an oxygen monitor on his foot, and the pinprick bruises on his left hand told of the several failed attempts to get an IV started. His right arm was plugged with the successfully inserted IV needle, and was strapped to a board the size of a generous nail file to keep it immobilized. His day old skin was stretched and bloody under the tape holding it all in place. A nurse stood over him, adjusting the dials on the equipment.

The hot tears sprang quickly to my eyes, obscuring my vision and threatening to spill out from their tenuous perches on my lower lids. I held them firmly in check; if my son could handle it, so could I.

"He's been fighting us!" the nurse remarked. "That's a good sign," she continued, "babies who are very sick don't fight back."

I was consumed with the urge to rip all the tubes

out and pick up my baby and run, but again, I was awed by his strength and followed his silent, stoic example.

"Hi my love," I said. Alex turned his head towards my voice and his eyelids fluttered as he tried to open them.

"Turning his head to Mama," the nurse crooned and smiled. "He recognizes your voice." This warmed my heart. Here was this tiny scrap of a boy, his age still counted in hours, who knew me above all others as his protector, his advocate, his mommy.

I slid a finger under the tent and touched his velvety arm. He flailed his arms and kicked his legs.

"He's so strong, he can really kick!" the nurse said.

"I know," I agreed, "I have the stretch marks to prove it!" We all chuckled. My husband and I stood over our son, listening to the beeps and bells ringing out every few seconds, keeping an eye on the monitors as the numbers rose and fell as erratically as his breath. "What do these numbers mean?" I asked the nurse. Of course I knew what a heart rate monitor was, but there were numbers I'd never seen, numbers I'd never cared to know about but would become intimately acquainted with as the night unfolded.

"These are his sats," the nurse explained, "His oxygen saturation levels. We want them in the 90s, and his keep dipping into the 80s when we take him off the oxygen." Another nurse materialized and told us we had to leave so that they could take chest Xrays. We retreated to our room to try and get some sleep.

Russell passed out on the couch, his long legs curled

as much as they could go in order to fit onto the cushions. I let several hours of broken and agitated rest go by. Finally, feeling completely helpless, I couldn't sit there any longer, and grunted with the effort to pull myself out of the bed. My fresh incision protested against the strain but I ignored it. I pulled on another hospital gown and managed to conceal enough of my bared flesh to be passable. I slowly shuffled back down to the nursery and got to the door just as the nurse was opening it.

"Would it be possible for me to hold my son?" I asked her.

She smiled. "I was just coming to get you!" she replied. "We want to try a little skin to skin." I didn't need much arm twisting; it had been hours since I'd held my baby. The nursery was very quiet; the calm broken only by an occasional cry from one of the hungry tykes in the bassinets or the whir of the air conditioner as it kicked in. I followed her to the back of the room, to the isolated bassinet under the heat lamp.

I had to wait while they put an oxygen tube into my baby's nose as they couldn't take him off the oxygen, and of course I couldn't hold him in the tent. He cried out angrily, his fists little balls of rage against the indignity of it all, tossing his head from side to side to avoid the tube. The nurse cut two tiny pieces of tape and stuck the tube down onto each of his cheeks to keep it in place.

One of the other staff had kindly pushed over an arm chair for me and I eased myself into it to get comfortable. As the nurse lifted Alex out of the bassinet I had sudden misgivings about holding him. There were so many wires and tubes and I didn't want to disturb them or hurt him. She gently untangled his legs and arms from the wires as she passed him over, and we had to do another intricate choreography of repositioning them as she laid him down onto my chest. I leaned back into the recliner, instantly feeling more at ease as my son curled into a little ball on my chest, his tiny hand on my shoulder.

The nurse and I watched the monitor intently, waiting with bated breath to see how this transfer would affect Alex's sats. His breathing calmed almost immediately, and I felt a strong sense of déjà vu, this contact is what had worked for Mia when she had too had had rapid respiration as a newborn. The nurse placed a receiving blanket over both of us and drew a curtain around us for some privacy.

I pulled one hand out from under the blanket and smoothed my child's little back and kissed his tiny head. His hair and skin felt like satin; I had forgotten how perfect newborn skin was. I saw the bruises on his little hands close up and they brought the tears to the precipices of my eyes all over again. My eyes were heavy with fatigue and my body was achy and stiff, but I willed my lids to stay up and opted not to pay any heed to the pain. We spent the next few hours like this, my boy and I, in a state of tranquil serenity at the back of the nursery.

Finally, when my heavy head could take it no longer

and I started to nod off, I reluctantly gave my soundly sleeping baby back to the nurse so that I didn't accidentally drop him, and returned to my room.

While I felt buoyed by this contact, Alex was not out of the woods yet, and we still didn't have a diagnosis. The xrays showed fluid on his lungs, so they had started him on antibiotics in case he had pneumonia. There wasn't a NICU at this hospital, but the nurses assured us that they were doing all they could, and that if a transport to a NICU did become necessary, my husband and I would be transported as well.

So it went over the next few days. My husband and I took turns sleeping and holding our baby, and Alex seemed to take one step forward and one step back. He would get to the point where he was able to breathe on his own, and then within the hour he was back on oxygen. He had a dedicated nurse day and night, someone keeping a constant vigil to make sure he was getting just the right amount of oxygen: too little could have serious consequences, but too much could mean permanent brain damage as well. To say these women were the epitome of compassion was a gross understatement. Their soothing, patient smiles kept me going, and they brought my lunches, dinners and medications to me in the nursery while I sat with Alex.

Our pediatrician stopped by every day to check in on Alex and reassured us that if he was *really* sick, they would have transported him to the NICU already. He diagnosed Alex with TTN – transient tachypnea of the newborn. Basically Alex's lungs didn't have enough surfactant for the alveoli to stay open, and they didn't absorb the fluid as they should have when he was born. It is unusual for a full term baby to have TTN; it is usually associated with preterm babies, not strapping almost 9 pounders who are delivered at 39 ½ weeks.

Mia and my parents came in each day to visit. She was perplexed as to where her baby brother was and why she couldn't see him. We told her he was sick and that he had to be in the nursery for a while, but wouldn't let her see him.

All we could do was wait.

Finally on the night before we were supposed to go home, it all caught up with me and I broke down. TTN usually goes away within 24 hours, but here we were, 4 days later, and Alex was still on oxygen, his sats and heart rate going up and down like the score of a complicated symphony. I stood, leaning against my husband who held me for a very long time, while I sobbed and begged God to heal my son and help him to breathe without assistance.

Later that night a pediatric respiratory therapist was called in. She brought with her a tiny cpap machine, the last ditch effort to try and solve this without having to send him on to a pediatric hospital.

She tried to hold the mask over Alex's face and he thrashed wildly, screaming in protest. His nurse held him down and the therapist began pumping. Every time she let up the mask, I could hear his screams anew, only for them to be drowned out as she resumed the rhythmic pushes. Finally, his yelling abated, and he fell asleep. The therapist pumped him with air for half an hour, and then took the mask off, revealing a deep imprint around his nose and mouth. But all was calm, and his breathing was even and strong.

We watched him, waiting for his sats to drop or his chest retractions to start back up but they didn't. He continued to sleep peacefully. The nurse swaddled him and placed him back in his basinet.

Half an hour went by. Then an hour. Then two. Alex was holding his own. I kissed my baby on his downy head and went back to my room to rest, finally able to breathe easily myself.

The pediatrician came by the next morning and gave Alex a clean bill of health. We would be able to take him home with us when we left that afternoon.

I gently placed Alex into the car seat and fumbled with the five point harness. It had been a long time since I'd put such a small baby into a car seat and I was even more nervous with him after what he'd just gone through. Even at 8 lbs 14 oz he looked so tiny in the seat, with his teeny hands resting on top of his miniscule knees, sleeping calmly in the snuggly infant positioner.

The dark bruises on his hands and the lipstick kiss of raw skin on his cheeks from where the tape had been were the only telltale signs of my baby's rough start. Yet none of it mattered now.

My boy was here and healthy and coming home.

THE WHEELS ON THE BUS

Wednesdays and Thursdays are Mia's "Daddy Days." My husband's changeling retail hours are typically all over the map, and while it means that schedule doesn't jive with my more traditional Saturdays and Sundays off, nine times out of ten these are the two days of the week when Mia can pretty much count on having her dad's undivided attention.

They also happen to be the days when her pre-Kindergarten class usually goes on field trips. I picked Mia up one afternoon and was regaled on the way home with much excitement about the upcoming trip to Safari Sam's and a pizza party. Safari Sam's is a Chuck E Cheese type of place with, as the name suggests, a safari theme.

"Wow, that sounds great!" I responded, "When are you going?"

She was a bit puzzled. "Hmmm, I don't know."

"I'll call and ask, ok?" I said, knowing that it was most likely going to happen on Wednesday or Thursday and that she was going to miss it. But I couldn't dash her hopes without at least an inquiry, and made a mental note to call the school.

Sure enough, when I called to find out about the excursion, the director confirmed that it was Thursday of that week.

"Oh, okay, thanks," I said, and was about to hang up.

"You can bring Mia if you want," the director offered. "She misses out on all these trips, and we won't charge her for the day, just the $5 fee for Safari Sam's," she added.

I was really touched by this. "Really? Thank you so much!" I said. "I know she would love to go!"

She gave me the details and we were all set.

Mia was elated. "I'll get to go on the BUS?!" she asked.

"Yes, love," I responded with a smile.

"Cool!!" she giggled, leaping up and down. Mia has been yearning to ride the bus like a "big kid" for ages. Her time had arrived.

Thursday morning came and I couldn't help notice the teeny knot in my stomach. As I got ready for work I reprimanded myself for being such an overprotective, worry wort of a mom, but couldn't shake the tiny siren in my head. It was like the squeaky buzz of the miniscule mosquitoes from my childhood as they hovered around my head on summer nights: not loud enough to move me to take action, but loud enough to be heard and distract my attention.

Mia bounded over to me as I sat down on the stairs to put my shoes on.

"Make sure you stay with your teacher at all times and don't talk to anyone you don't know," I said.

"Okay Mommy, I will," she pacified me.

We wrapped our arms around each other and I felt the intoxicating rush of love that happens every time we hug. Still squeezing, I said, "I love you with my whole heart, pumpkin."

"I love you too, Mommy," she beamed as she pulled away.

I looked into her bright eyes, inches from mine. What I wanted to say was DON'T GO! Stay here with Daddy!! Don't take your eyes off your teacher for a second!! Make sure you stay with your group so you don't get lost!! Are you SURE you wouldn't rather stay home with Daddy so I know where you are?!?

"Have lots of fun today, I can't wait to hear all about your trip when I pick you up!" was what I managed instead, and gave her another hug, hoping I had disguised enough of the terror in my voice to sound convincing.

"Thanks Mom!" she smiled. "Have a good day at work."

With that, I headed out the door to face the back to back meeting marathon that awaited me at the office, still trying to shush that persistent alarm ringing in the back of my thoughts.

Quitting time couldn't come fast enough and I made my way over to the little school house to pick up my daughter.

"So, there's something I need to tell you," began the teacher at the front desk. She must have noticed my eyes widen, or perhaps she could actually see my heart thudding out of my chest because she quickly added, "Everything's fine, but the bus broke down on the way to Safari Sam's today. The police came and escorted the kids across the road to wait until the new bus got there. I just wanted you to be aware of what happened."

"Oh alright, thanks for letting me know," I said as nonchalantly as I could, grateful for the honesty but at the same time, thinking that maybe this was something I really didn't want to know.

All the horrific incidents one hears or reads about whizzed through my head... the eighteen kids who died in a crash when the school bus careened off the road, a drunk driver who lost control of her car and plowed into the group of children waiting at the bus stop, the teenager in my driver's ed class who was nabbed for speeding past a school bus that was stopped with its red lights flashing and stop sign out.

Of course, to keep this in perspective, it was just a broken down bus, and my daughter had the watchful eye of not only her teachers but the police as well. None of the kids had a scratch on them and they were returned safely by the end of the day, having had a great time.

I am aware that I can't change my daughter's name to Rapunzel and hide her away somewhere. I want her to have the full gamut of experiences I had as a child, and live enough to have memories that will be worthy of reminiscing about when she's looking back in another eighty years.

In the end, my purpose as her mother is to arm her with the information she needs to be as safe as possible, empower her as best I can and then as all parents eventually do, let her go.

Yet while I know she isn't mine to keep, Mia will always be my baby. Unlike the plastic monitor I used for the first few years of her life, the one inside my heart can never be switched off. As long as there is breath in my body it will always be on, tuned into a frequency that only a mother's intuition can hear.

I recall how I used to laugh at moms who cried after seeing their children off on their first day of Kindergarten. I can only hope that on that day in September later this year, one of them will be gracious enough to pass me the tissues.

OUR AUSTRALIA

"So, how do you feel about moving to Oregon?" I asked my husband. My heart was thudding a little in my ears. This was the man who had had a fit when I moved the couch from one side of the living room to the other. He was someone who stood in one place for two minutes and started growing roots. In fact, he was such a creature of habit that I had contemplated not even asking him.

But we were so desperate that I couldn't not ask this incredibly important question.

I honestly believed that would be the end of the conversation. However, to my complete shock and total amazement, my husband replied, "Well, let's think about it."

My husband was laid off at the time and I had just found out that I was going to be losing my job as well. After they told me, I spent the afternoon sobbing in one of the stalls of the bathroom at work. We were thousands and thousands of dollars in debt and now we were both going to be unemployed. Our impoverished financial situation was causing terrible tension between us and we had massive rows over anything that required spending money: going out to a movie, buying that extra bag of chips at the grocery store, meeting a friend for coffee. We were a few paychecks away from sleeping on a park bench.

My long distance workmates in the Oregon office had casually mentioned that there were open positions and inquired if I would be interested in one of them. Moving eight hundred miles had never been part of the plan, but then nothing else was going according to plan, either.

Over the next few weeks, we kept our seesaw of indecision to ourselves. Our lives were in LA. Did we throw in the towel or try and make it work there? It got to the point where we literally sat down one night and made a pros and cons list. Promising each other to be very neutral and objective, we started with the cons to leaving: family, friends, sunshine. Then we began working on the pros: forty two percent lower cost of living, at least one of us employed, a chance to pay off our debt, an hour from the mountains, beach and skiing, washing machines in each apartment unit. As the list quickly outgrew the cons, we had our answer.

Yet, neither one of us was ready to speak it out loud, neither had the guts to call it.

The days sludged on and it came time to make a decision, either way. I had been offered the position and it wouldn't hold forever.

It was late. My husband and I were poring over the apartment guide magazines my Oregon work buddies, aka the "Lure Romi to Oregon Committee" had nonchalantly sent us as bait. Neither of us spoke for a long while.

It was Russell who broke the silence. "I think you're going to Oregon with or without me."

I looked up to meet his deep, calm, blue eyes. This statement wasn't said in anger; it was merely an observation. Once again, my husband's acute intuitiveness had homed in to the basic truth. In my immaturity, and to spare his feelings, I couldn't bring myself to admit it so I brightly assured him that wasn't the case. But his hunch haunted me; we both knew in our bones that he was right.

We attempted to sleep on it that night, but neither of us got a wink. The next day at work, my cell phone rang. It was Russell.

"Take the job," he said. "Whatever they offer you, I think we should go."

"Are you sure?" I said, giving us one last out.

"Yes," he reaffirmed. "Let me know what they say. I love you."

I could feel a slow smile spread across my face. "I love you too."

My heart was pounding again. I dialed my future boss and told her I would accept her offer. We chatted about some of the logistics and agreed on a salary. I was furiously excited, nervous, numb, delirious. It was done. We were moving to Portland.

My parents told me that when I was two and my mom was pregnant with my brother, a man had offered my father a job in Australia. He told him to get to Melbourne and he would take care of the rest. My mom couldn't reconcile herself with moving halfway around the world with one child and another on the way, on an offer at a cocktail party. They made the choice to stay in South Africa and we eventually moved to Cincinnati, Ohio instead.

Australia became our synonym for the promised land, the choices we are given in life and the chances we choose to take.

We left LA on February 2nd, 2002. Somewhere around San Francisco I felt a queasy panic and wanted to turn around at the next off-ramp and head back south on the 5. But my foot stayed steady on the gas pedal and before I knew it, we were rounding breathtaking Mount Shasta, its snow-capped peak jutting out magnificently against the brilliant turquoise sky. There were traces of snow on the ground but the roads were totally clear. It was as if the Universe was gently shuttling us along, encouraging us in hushed whispers audible only to our intuition that we were doing the right thing.

By the time we snaked our way through the misty hills of Ashland, I felt a building sense of anticipation, a growing effervescence bubbling up in the very air I breathed.

*****

February 2nd, 2009, exactly seven years after Russell and I took our leap of faith, I watched our three year old daughter through the big window of the Honeycomb room at her daycare center. She was sitting at one of the tables, her chestnut ringlets cascading down her back and over her face. Only her cheeks were visible from my vantage point, and her head was tilted to the left in concentration. I followed her miniature arm down to her chubby fingers and found they were wrapped around a pencil, drawing a picture.

I entered the room and went to sit quietly beside her. She looked up and her hazel eyes sparkled as she dazzled me with a huge grin. I kissed the top of her head and put my arm around her little shoulders.

"Look Mommy, I made a picture of you!" she beamed. Her purple rendering had a wobbly, oblong head, huge round eyes complete with shaky irises and pupils, a wide, friendly smile, arms, legs and dashes on the top for hair.

I swallowed a little lump in my throat and smiled at my daughter through filmy eyes. Just seven years after we'd left LA on the verge of divorce and destitution, my husband and I had paid off every dollar of our tens of thousands worth of debt, bought a car, bought a house, been promoted nine times between us, gone on several vacations, and borne a little girl more beautiful, witty, sweet and loving than we could ever have imagined.

We had taken the chance and the what if was better

than we could have asked for.

This was our second chance. Our Australia.

WHAT WOULD YOU LIKE TO EAT TODAY?

"Hello, what would you like to eat today?" My pint sized waitress was looking at me expectantly, notepad in one hand and pen poised over it in the other.

I switched immediately into customer mode; we were evidently playing restaurant. My daughter gestured for me to sit down on the cushion on the floor that was situated in front of several little plastic plates and cups.

"I would like a salad please," I responded, trying not to grunt as I heaved my eight month pregnant belly down onto the cushion and tried to get comfortable.

"Mmm, hmm," she murmured, as she scribbled down some squiggles on her note pad. "We have salad with chicken, or mango or tuna."

I pondered that for a moment. "The mango sounds good, I'd like the one with mango please."

"Okay." More scribbling. "What dressing would you like?"

"No dressing, thank you, just some lemon," I

ordered.

"No, pretend you want some dressing," she corrected me.

My daughter has no respect for the golden rule of improv.

If my answer is not to her liking, she has no qualms about steering me in a more pleasing direction. She has often been known to feed me several of my lines at a time, which much to her chagrin, I invariably forget or flub horribly, leading to a chorus of exasperated sighs and eye rolling from Her Directorship.

"I'd love some dressing," I tried again, "What would you recommend?"

"Well, we have ranch, chocolate strawberry or one with lemons and coconut," she said.

"I think I'll just have some ranch, please," I selected.

"Are you sure you wouldn't like the one with chocolate and strawberry?" she tried to upsell.

"I'm quite sure, thank you," I affirmed, "And can you please put that on the side?"

"No problem!" she cooed, and recorded my satisfactory choice on her notepad. "Do you have a daughter?" I have tried to say no on previous occasions, but have not yet been allowed to dine alone. I know the answer to this question is an unwavering yes.

"I do," I confirmed.

"And what would she like?" Mia inquired. "We have mac and cheese, grilled cheese and pisgetti."

I turned to the vacant spot to my right. I waited for my imaginary daughter to make up her mind. "She'd like the mac and cheese, please," I ordered for her.

"Mac and cheese," Mia nodded approvingly. "And what would she like to drink? We have lemonade, orange juice, milk and water."

"She likes orange juice," I said and held my breath for the retort.

"Pretend she wants to try the lemonade," Mia said, right on cue.

"But she doesn't like lemonade," I said, breaking character along with her for a moment.

"Pretend you tell her she has to try it, she might liiiiiike it!" Mia reminded me.

There was only one way to play this hand and we both knew it. "Let's try the lemonade, you might like it," I told my invisible offspring.

Mia moved on. "And what would your husband like?

"Honey, what would you like?" I asked the empty spot on the other side of the cushion. My legs were going numb so I shifted a bit on the cushion. I waited the obligatory amount of time for my "husband" to peruse the menu. "He would like the steak, please, and a side of veggies."

"Oh," she said apologetically, "We're out of steaks." I looked over and shot my husband the 'oh well, what now' face.

"What do you have instead?" I asked.

"Let me check with serfice," she said. "Serfice!" She looked back towards the play kitchen in the living room. "What else do we have?"

Service ran through the other choices from the kitchen, while she listened intently.

"We have shrimp," she finally announced. "That comes with peas and carrots and grapes."

I waited patiently for my ethereal other half to yay or nay this replacement. "That sounds great, thank you, he'll have the shrimp."

"Of course," she said jovially, jotted down a few more notes on her notepad and let me know she'd be over at the kitchen or waiting on the other customers if I needed anything. This was my prompt to need something. Dining at this establishment in the past has taught me that such an offer was an expectation requiring follow up as opposed to a casual comment.

I watched her describing the daily delectables to the table next to me. She was very professional and efficient. It was obvious she had been scrutinizing our interactions with wait staff quite carefully, as she was actually really good at this! I gave her a few seconds more to walk back to the kitchen to place their order. "Excuse me?" I ventured. She poked her head around from the fridge door, grabbing her notepad and pen. "May I please have something to drink for myself?"

"Oh yes!" came the prompt reply. "We have tea that comes with coconut in it, or coke… or lemonade… or water."

"I'll have water please," I replied.

"Oh, sorry, we're out of water," she countered.

"Out of water?!" I exclaimed. "How do you wash the dishes then?"

"We have that kind of water," she said, without missing a beat. "We just don't have the kind for drinking."

"Hmm…okay…well then I guess I'll have a coke please."

"Coming up!" she chirped and disappeared into the kitchen. By this stage my legs were completely numb and I really needed to stand up.

When she got back with the coke, she asked if I had a pet with me. I was about to tell her I would never dream of bringing my dog into a restaurant, and then realized that of course, I had obviously forgotten about the large canine seated under our table.

"Yes, I brought my dog in with us," I said. She gave me a sympathetic smile.

"We have a no pet policy here," she informed me. "Your dog will have to wait outside."

I told the errant pooch he was going to have to go, and asked how much I owed her for the meal. The sumptuous repast came to only $4, which in my opinion, was quite a bargain for such attentive serfice.

I picked up a cardboard clothes tag that was within arm's reach to suffice as a credit card, which she expertly ran through the cash register and then gave me a $5 bill as change. My waitress was a little miffed when I grabbed her and gave her a big hug and a kiss on her delicious cheeks but I couldn't help myself.

"Please come back and visit another day," she wrapped up our interaction as I tottered upright.

"I definitely will," I reassured her, and was about to

add another thought, but she was already busily listening to her next customer, notepad ready and pen poised to capture all the particulars and offer some recommendations as only she can.

NOT YOUR AVERAGE LION

A hot, irritated sigh shot out of my lips as I flapped the instruction page of the cardboard cake pop stand over again. I took another look at the center column balancing precariously in my left hand and then consulted the directions. Again. I had now slid the halves over the middle and attempted to insert them into the slots as shown. For the thirty ninth time. Yet there was still a 2 inch gap between the two pieces. How was the cardboard going to lock when the two halves didn't even touch?!

I turned the statuette over and over, fumbling desperately to get the cardboard to line up so that I could force the little tabs into the unwilling slots. The cardboard was splitting now, and each time I tried to jam it into the ill-fitting space it separated a little more, thus becoming progressively weakened. ARRRRRRRRGH! I took a deep, furious breath and closed my eyes. Upon opening them I spied the rest of the cardboard layers in the pile and realized I was working with the wrong sized set of base pieces. With renewed energy I picked up the larger discs and they slid between the much abused slots with little effort. I put the remaining pieces together and was a bit shocked when the whole thing came together quite sturdily.

Now all that was left, at this obscene hour the night before my daughter's sixth birthday party, was to extricate the blessed cake pops from the pan, dip them into the candy coating, roll them in the sprinkles and call it a night. This task, having been started at ten past procrastination earlier that evening had already been waylaid several times by my five month old son, who decided it was the perfect night for a sleep strike.

Naturally the cake pops my daughter and I baked just for the fun of it on a random weekend several weeks prior had all practically fallen out of the pan as perfectly round, fluffy spheres. As the self-proclaimed new master of popology, I didn't entertain the idea that beginner's luck might have had a hand to play in this. So, par for the course, this time when I attempted to separate the top of the pan from the bottom, every pop disintegrated into a crumbly explosion of cake carnage. I had no backup plan. I had to forge ahead. I googled cake pop recipes and to my good fortune, found that all the recipes called for a baked cake, crumbled, and then mixed with a can of frosting. Excellent! So really, I was just a step ahead of myself.

I ran upstairs to let my husband know I was stepping out to go to the grocery store.

"Do you need anything?" I offered, "I'm going to the store quickly."

His forehead scrunched in surprise. It was late. Really late. "What are you getting at the store?" he asked quizzically

"Frosting," I confessed. He sighed.

"Why do you do this to yourself?"

"Because I am an idiot."

"Next year... BUY. A. CAKE." He shook his head. It was a familiar shake. As usual it was accompanied by a look that was an interesting combination of disbelief and resignation.

As I took my crumb-encrusted, flour-dusted self off to the store, I began to think. Why *do* I do this to myself? Why is it not good enough to just order a cake from the bakery like a normal person? Why must I sit up the night before anything, battling to finish the handmade, one of a kind, hair-brained idea du jour?

And the answer came to me. Each woman who answers to the sing-songed title of Mommy must also become a resident expert in everything. To name a very small few, hats such as Expert Spider Killer Extraordinaire, Boo Boo Bandaider, Enthusiastic Story Reader, and Artful Food Presentation That Looks Like A Face So That Your Kids Will Actually Eat the Veggies Coordinator hang outside the proverbial office of each of these hulking superwomen.

In addition to the titles she acquires slowly and steadily – aka Changer of the Diaper of the Child While She's Standing, Silent Slinker From the Room After Rocking the Baby to Sleep for an Hour so that You Don't Wake Him Again, and Doer of Everything With

205

One Hand While You Hold the Baby In The Other- a mother must also face those that demand to be mastered immediately, such as Activities With the Stuffed Animal Brought Home in a Bag From School for the Night With No Notice Journaler, Your Child Had a Bad Day at School Cheerer Upper, and Can I Have a Third Cookie Approver or Decliner.

When I became pregnant with my first child, I expected that upon reaching motherhood I would snap back to my usual self pretty much immediately, just with the addition of a child to look after. From being able to wear my pre-pregnancy clothes a week after delivery to emerging from the pregnancy fog and regaining my memory mere seconds after the doctor cut the umbilical cord, the fantastical version of my maternal self was boundless in both physical and mental strength and energy.

The truth, however, despite what the stories about the mombots in the media would have you believe, is that being a mother in our modern times is nothing short of a herculean feat. The pressure is intense, and it doesn't let up for an instant. My mom and I were discussing this very thing and she made a really valid point.

"Look at animals," she explained. "Take lion mothers for example. They just lie around calmly on the plains and their babies come and go and feed as they need to. They don't have to go to work or do the dishes. They only have to take care of their cubs."

Bingo.

Sure, I don't have to kill an antelope or zebra on a fairly frequent basis. However, mommy lions don't have to remember to make appointments for their children's well child exams, dental checkups, or haircuts. They don't have bills to pay, or checkbooks to balance, or cars that have to be taken in for oil changes every three thousand miles. They don't have to make school lunches or do the laundry or mop the floors. I have yet to hear about a mommy lion who needs to read to her kindergartener for 30 minutes each evening, or supervise homework while she is trying to put together a nutritious meal for her kids after arriving home at six o'clock at night, having picked them up from daycare immediately following a ten hour work day.

On the weekends, mommy lions do not need to arrange play dates or take their young to karate or art class or science class. They do not need to remember the birthdays of all the other lions around them, or store social security numbers, passwords, login IDs, immunization records and a running list of who refuses to eat what anymore in their moggy mommy minds.

Mommy lions aren't expected to work out like fiends or wear suffocating garments that cause them to get lightheaded in order to suck in their rolls to get their post-baby bodies to look like those of teenage boys.

They do not have to subject themselves to eyebrow waxes. Mommy lions aren't scolded by the magazine headlines in the grocery store checkout lines for letting themselves go.

Nobody makes disparaging comments to mommy

lions for having a messy house or car filled with their children's crap that seems to multiply exponentially as if by mitosis each day. Mommy lions do not have gardens to weed, mow and deadhead, rhizomes to divide or hedges to trim.

Mommy lions do not have to try and keep rowdy cubs quiet while they sit on conference calls at 5:00am, or work from 6:00am to 5:00pm sometimes without a break and stay up until 11:00pm so that they can answer the emails they should have been answering between the aforementioned hours. The friends of mommy lions do not judge them for falling behind on answering their emails or failing to check messages on Facebook.

Needless to say, this is enough to make the average person question their worth, not to mention sanity, on any given day.

This is why I nearly destroy myself to do better than good enough: so that I might for once feel like I *can* do it all; so that I can pretend I'm still the capable human being I once was who actually got things done. By constantly attempting to top myself I compensate for my shortcomings as a mother, and for the fact that I am struggling to do my best yet missing the mark more times than my bruised pride would like to allow.

Finally, almost drunk with exhaustion, having married the frosting and cake remains into dense little morsels that were all rolled, dipped and sprinkled and put to bed in the fridge, I dragged my aching bones upstairs to check on my children.

My daughter was sprawled across the bed, her limbs

splayed out from under a giant ball of duvet. A tiny smile flickered at the corners of her mouth, her face the very picture of serenity. I kissed her lightly on her forehead and crept out of her room.

Across the hallway, I opened the door to my infant son's room ever so gingerly and stood by his crib.

My baby's arms were both stretched out to the side, his tiny, chubby hands relaxed with his palms facing up. His deliciously plump legs, usually going a mile a minute, were still and calm. His impossibly long lashes cast shadows down his rosy round cheeks in the warm glow of the nightlight, and his fuzzy little head was turned ever so slightly toward me.

I may not be a perfect mom. I may never have a spotless house, or get the kids' school photos mailed out to all the relatives on time, or get rid of my postpartum muffin top. But I love my babies with a gigantic, bottomless heart, and, in spite of all my imperfections, they love me equally in return.

I can't think of anything more perfect than that.

ACKNOWLEDGEMENTS

A huge thank you to Jennifer Redmond, Amy Hansen and Heidi Carter for their mentorship and editing which shaped this book into what it finally became, and to my family and friends who tirelessly read the barrage of pieces in varying states of readiness and gave me much needed feedback.

Thank you Jennifer Margolis and my good natured little model for braving the elements to get the perfect cover shot.

Thank you Ron Valiente for all the technical support.

To my own parents, thank you for everything, you made it all look so effortless!

Thank you to my husband and my children, for your unwavering support, and for sharing me with the laptop all those nights so that I could finish this book. I love you!

www.ingramcontent.com/pod-product-compliance
Lightning Source LLC
Chambersburg PA
CBHW051724040426
42447CB00008B/963